THE DOLLAR DEFICIT
DEFICIT
Causes and Cures

Edited with Introductions by
H. PETER GRAY
WAYNE STATE UNIVERSITY

D. C. HEATH AND COMPANY · BOSTON

CONTENTS

iii

INTRODUCTION

International transactions, like all economic dealings, usually do (and are always expected to) benefit both the seller and the buyer, or they would not be made. Ordinarily what is good for the individual is also good for society, so that the nation as a whole benefits from international trade. These gains from trade can be seen in the enjoyment of goods and services which could not be produced at home, in the enjoyment of goods and services which can be obtained from abroad more cheaply than they can be produced at home, and from the weakening by foreign competition of any monopolistic strength enjoyed by a domestic industry. Unfortunately, the gains from trade are not acquired without some cost on the part of individuals. Some individuals suffer economically because their skills and/or products are competitive with those of foreigners and their incomes are reduced as a result of foreign competition *in their particular market*. Other individuals possess skills or goods which foreigners cannot supply at the going price; in the absence of international trade these people would be less well off because of the reduced effective demand for their skills and goods. The gains and losses by individuals, however, are the result of the global allocation of resources by the market mechanism and, as such, are of little concern. Individual costs are more than offset by the gains of the main body of consumers within the same society.

The international market mechanism is not perfect. The imperfections will benefit some and penalize others. The most common imperfection is a tariff or quota: this measure taxes a foreign product and thus accords an advantage to the domestic producer. The cost of the imperfection is borne by the domestic consumer and the foreign producer and the benefit acquired by the domestic industry. International imperfections of this kind are a part of commercial policy and, in addition to their effects on individuals, they also affect the general conditions of trade among nations (the terms of trade), usually according an advantage to the tariff-imposing nation at the expense of other nations.

The other major source of costs from international trade stems from the need for a nation to balance its international accounts. A nation is an economic unit in the international market and therefore must limit its expenditures in foreign currencies to its earnings and net borrowings of foreign currency. This need to balance its accounts stems from the fact that different national currencies are involved and, if the price of one currency in terms of the other is to remain unchanged, the amount of a currency offered must be matched by the amount demanded. Clearly, if the relative prices of the two currencies are not to remain fixed and if the price effect on the demand for internationally-traded goods is sufficiently great, a system of flexible exchange-rates between national currencies will ensure balance in the international accounts of all nations.

The current international monetary mechanism is characterized by virtually fixed rates of exchange among national currencies. The rates are kept within one percent of the par value of each currency by the relevant monetary authority, which offsets market pressures by buying or selling foreign currency. These foreign currency operations of the monetary authorities are conducted out of a national stock of international reserves (gold and foreign currency holdings). Moreover, this stock may be temporarily augmented by loans from the International Monetary Fund or other monetary authorities. In cases of extreme difficulty, a change in the par value of a currency is permitted.

Since the international transactions of the United States are conducted largely by corporations and individuals, there is no *a priori* reason (in the short run) to expect that the sum total of debits (sales of dollars) will automatically equal the credit total (purchases of dollars) during a calendar year. In this case, an *imbalance* of payments will have occurred and the intervention of the monetary authority will be necessary if the foreign exchange market is to clear itself. The imbalance will be an economist's concept of imbalance and not an accounting imbalance, which is not possible with a system of double-entry bookkeeping. The reconciliation between the economist's and the accountant's concept of balance is achieved by the addition to or subtraction from the liquid reserve position of the monetary authority. Since a deficit results in a decline in the international reserve position of the monetary authority, a series of continuous deficits is a matter of national concern since continual reductions inevitably result in the eventual depletion of the stock of national reserves. Therefore a series of deficits in the international accounts requires that something be done to correct the underlying causes of the deficit. It is in this corrective action that the cost of international trade is likely to occur, since there is very likely to be a conflict between the nation's domestic economic goals of full employment and stable prices and balance in the international payments.

The United States Balance of Payments

Since the Korean War, the United States has run a deficit in its international accounts in every year but one.[1] Until 1958, these deficits were

---

[1] Balance-of-payments data are published regularly in detail in the Department of Commerce's *Survey of Current Business* and in abbreviated form in the *Federal Reserve Bulletin*.

small and intentional: small because of the exaggerated demand for American goods resulting from the slow recovery of the European productive capacity after the war, and intentional because of the need for the United States to reduce its disproportionate share of the world's gold stock. In 1958, the European recovery was largely complete and the international reserves of the European nations had attained a more satisfactory level. Hence, intentional deficits ceased to be a policy objective on the part of the United States.

Instead of the elimination of the small deficit, the change in policy produced a substantial increase in the size of the deficit and no immediate prospects for its reduction. Since this time, the official United States policy has been to reduce and eventually to eliminate the deficit. An official policy devoted to the reduction of a deficit eliminates any possibility of allowing the slow-working mechanism of market forces to cure the deficit. Thus, the United States Government was committed by its support of the existing international monetary mechanism to the maintenance of the gold parity of the dollar, (i.e., depreciation of the U.S. dollar is not a permissible alternative), and to positive action to reduce a deficit.

The Problem of Measurement

The question of what constitutes a deficit or a surplus in a nation's international accounts is not beyond dispute. Multiple concepts exist and the first selection in this volume is devoted to the measurement of the United States deficits under alternative definitions.[2] Since that paper was written an alternative definition has been evolved by the Review Committee for Balance of Payments Statistics, appointed to investigate the reliability of the U.S. data on international trade.[3] Since the Committee's definition will be officially reported on a regular basis, the concept must be outlined here.

In addition to problems of the quality of the underlying data, the Committee addressed itself to the crucial problem of defining a measure of imbalance. There is a need by policy-influencing economists and politicians for numerical summary indicators of the nation's international position, even though the individual indicator must always be used in the full awareness of its derivation. The measure given principal emphasis in official publications for the last ten years has been the "balance on regular types of transactions." This measure is based on a liquidity concept which in turn stems from the belief that the use of the dollar as an international trading currency is based upon its convertibility into gold. Therefore, this measure emphasizes the banker's attitude and concerns itself with the juxtaposition of liquid assets and liquid liabilities and of

[2] "Measurement of a Nation's Balance of Payments."

[3] *The Balance of Payments Statistics of the United States, A Review and Appraisal*, Report of the Review Committee for Balance of Payments Statistics to the Bureau of the Budget, April 1965.

changes in these quantities. Long-term transactions are separated from sales and purchases of gold and from transactions in short-term claims, and the deficit is defined as the sum of the net increase in short-term liabilities to foreigners and the net decrease in monetary assets. In place of this definition, the Committee proposed that the deficit be measured by the "official settlements" concept. This concept attempts to measure the amount of official intervention in the foreign exchange markets which is necessary to maintain the value of the currency within the prescribed limits, *i.e.*, the amount of official funds required to offset a spontaneously occurring imbalance in the foreign-exchange market.

In its essentials, the controversy between the two concepts turns on the treatment of any increase in short-term dollar claims of foreigners other than foreign monetary authorities — foreign commercial banks, private citizens, and international nonmonetary institutions, etc. If any increase in United States liabilities to such foreign creditors is seen as showing a spontaneous desire on the part of these creditors to hold dollars as an asset, then clearly any increase in these assets is a spontaneous or autonomous one and may legitimately be treated as an offset to autonomous acquisitions of long-term foreign assets by United States residents. If the further assumption is made, as it is by both concepts, that changes in foreign official holdings are made in response to imbalances, then the official settlements concept accurately measures any weakness of the dollar in foreign exchange markets. If, on the other hand, the increase in liabilities in the accounts of foreign commercial banks is a result of requests made to these foreign banks by foreign monetary authorities responding to a plea for cooperation by the Board of Governors of the Federal Reserve System, the increase in liabilities to private foreigners is merely an increase in official holdings in a different guise. In that case, the increase should not be counted as a spontaneous financing of a deficit on current and on long-term capital account. Therefore the increase in liabilities should be included in the measurement of the deficit.

In neither definition is the increase in short-term foreign assets held by United States residents deemed anything but an autonomous outflow of dollars which must be financed. The underlying argument is that monetary authorities of the United States do not possess the legal powers to require that such funds be repatriated in response to a national need to defend the dollar. For this reason such assets cannot legitimately be regarded as reserves. Foreign claims on the United States can be cashed at any time and must therefore be treated — from the banking point of view — as potential claims on the gold stock.

The question of the correctness of either definition hinges upon which relationship is important at the time and upon the relationships between foreign official monetary authorities and their private monetary institutions. No clear-cut answer is available, but protagonists of the liquidity concept are keenly aware of potential withdrawals and argue that the acquisition of funds which can be withdrawn at negligible notice cannot realistically be regarded as spontaneous financing of a deficit on current and long-term capital account. An excellent rebuttal to criticism of the official settlements concept is given by Edward M. Bernstein in a supplement to Part Three of the official *Hearings* on the *Report* before the Joint Economic Committee's Subcommittee on Economic Statistics.[4] Neither measure is ideal, but the official settlements concept is more likely to answer the question relevant to policy decisions most of the time.

The official estimate of the deficit is an important figure because the U.S. dollar is a key currency in world trade and is held as an asset by many nations. The official estimate of the deficit affects the confidence of foreign dollar holders in the ability of the United States to maintain the convertibility of the dollar into gold at the existing parity. This confidence is itself vital to the continued role of the dollar as an international medium of exchange, and no satisfactory substitute exists. The official settlements definition does reduce the official deficit for every year since 1954 and its adoption should allay any lack of confidence in the dollar (except that creditors are naturally suspicious of a change in a yardstick in times of stress). The main virtue of the official settlements concept is that it denotes the strength or weakness of the dollar in current foreign exchange markets better than any other single summary indicator and therefore will preclude an unnecessarily restrictive bias being given to official policy.

The other important contribution of the Committee was a detailed investigation of the means of generating the actual statistics that constitute or underlie the international accounts of the United States. It stressed the potential inaccuracy of the data and emphasized the need for qualitatively better data as a basis for policy decisions. Almost inevitably the required improvement in the quality of the data requires more expensive methods of data generation and estimation, but the irrationality of forming economic policy on the basis of potentially unreliable data is self-evident. Refusal by the Congress to appropriate the necessary funds will be misplaced parsimony indeed.

The Problem of Feedback

It is a simple task to examine balance of payments data, to observe those component items which have deteriorated and to identify these items as the cause of the deficit or of its increase. Unfortunately, this procedure offers no real explanation of the cause of changes in the net balance. Because of the complex interrelationships between the various items in the accounts, such an explanation would not be valid. The effect on the net balance of a change in imports of one item can be judged only by analyzing the way in which the change affects other items in the balance of payments and *not* by its impact upon the net balance of its own individual account. Consider a commodity, X, which is both exported and

4 June 9, 1965, pp. 286–289.

imported by the United States — imports exceeding exports so that the particular account shows a deficit. The imposition by the U.S. of a tax on imports of X will, if demand is not inelastic, reduce expenditures on imports of X before payment of duty. The reduced expenditures on imports will lessen the income of foreign suppliers of X and, in the absence of stimulatory measures by foreign authorities, the demand for American exports will be reduced. Since the foreign currency earnings of other nations will have been reduced, stimulatory measures by foreign authorities will not follow automatically. Thus the imposition of a tax on X will have the direct effect of reducing imports of X and the indirect effect of reducing the demand for United States exports.[5] The income effect on the foreign demand for Americans goods will be transmitted to the markets for these exports through the interaction of myriads of market forces in the rest of the world as the suppliers of X reduce their expenditures in accordance with their individual preference patterns. Assuming a stable system and no retaliation, the income effect on exports will, in the absence of price effects, be smaller than the original reduction in American imports and the reduction in imports by foreigners will be distributed throughout the whole range of American export goods. The absolute improvement in the net balance on the account for X will exaggerate the improvement in the balance on current account induced by the imposition of the tax.

The idea of feedback is a simple one. The decision to open a manufacturing plant abroad will occasion a debit in the form of a capital export, but the capital export will bring about the export of machinery to the new factory. The foreign aid program will also generate capital exports and countervailing exports of goods and services. Ordinary imports by the United States will increase the ability of the exporting nation to buy American-made goods; thus the net effect of an additional import will be smaller than the value of that import. Similarly, some exports incorporate imported materials so that an increase in such exports necessarily engenders an increase in imports.

In addition to these types of feedback, there are other kinds which act less directly and, probably, more slowly. Direct foreign investment (−) may lead to the repatriation of profits (+), the export of raw materials or semi-manufactures (+), the displacement of exports to the nation in which the manufacturing capacity was located (−), the displacement of exports to other nations (−), the payment of royalty and patent fees (+), etc. Similarly, the more simple type of feedback which occurs when an import from a nation results in increased exports to that country, can be more complex: the effects of the increased imports may be spread throughout many countries which in turn increase their imports until some increase in American exports eventually occurs. Finally, not all

[5] For simplicity it is assumed that no complementary or substitute goods are traded internationally.

feedbacks need be offsetting: some may enhance the original flow, for example, a tourist taking a foreign liner.

This complex interplay of international transactions precludes simplistic statements as to the cause or the cure of the American deficit. However, the concept of feedback does offer a crucial guide to policymakers: the first sectors to be considered for curbing are those with the smallest feedback. Unfortunately, there is no foolproof rule which states that all entries in item A have smaller feedbacks than all entries in item B. But it is possible to deduce the average, approximate feedback effects for types of transactions and for certain areas — some of which may have smaller feedbacks than others for a given type of transaction. While the idea of maximizing the saving of foreign exchange per dollar of frustrated transaction is appealing and maximizing feedback would be an efficient method of distinguishing between sectors, such a policy is dangerous. Traditionally the United States has not discriminated among nations in its international economic relations and the United States is committed to the continuance of this policy by its agreements with its fellow member nations in O.E.C.D. To the extent that efficient interference means eliminating imports from Country A, it is not possible. However, it is possible to restrict imports of a good for which Country A is the main supplier. But such measures are likely to produce countermeasures and are also likely to have unfortunate political repercussions. The severity of the principle of nondiscrimination is much smaller when capital transactions are concerned and this may be the reason that the emphasis of governmental interference in international transactions in defense of the dollar have tended to concentrate on capital exports — discriminating mainly against developed nations.

The Individual Accounts

Since 1958, the United States has achieved in every year a surplus on current account, *i.e.,* the value of the goods and services sold exceeds the value of goods and services purchased. This surplus would, in the absence of other items show that the United States had been "paying its way." However, in some years the surplus was so small as to justify the statement that a deficit on current account would have resulted had it not been for the export stimuli given by private capital exports and foreign aid.

On average, the United States has achieved a surplus on goods and services which has been more than offset by the deficit on capital account. The situation may therefore be summarized by the statement that "the dollar deficit of the United States has been caused, not by living beyond one's means, but by investing beyond one's means." The deficits on private capital accounts and government account have exceeded the surplus achieved through trade. Thus the argument can be, and is, made that the United States does not have a balance of payments problem but a liquidity problem.

The difficulty of reducing such a deficit is manifest. The political situation is such that government expenditures abroad cannot be further reduced nor their feedback increased. Private capital cannot be controlled without serious domestic opposition and renunciation of the basic economic principle of the free movement of capital and, in the absence of voluntary cooperation by business, without a whole superstructure of bureaucratic supervision. Certainly voluntary programs of restraint of capital movements seem a normal first step, but the more conscientious the businessman and the greater his awareness of the social benefit, the less conscientiously is he serving his stockholders. Additionally, business is not ordinarily able to reduce its foreign investment plans marginally: a decision to reduce direct investment could mean the elimination of an undertaking *in toto*. There are, however, two possible ways in which business may effect marginal savings in foreign currency without severely limiting their freedom of action: one is to repatriate an increased proportion of profits on foreign investments and the other is to finance any opening or expansion of foreign facilities to a much greater degree by borrowing in overseas capital markets — the smaller the feedback, the greater the proportion of capital funds which should be borrowed abroad.

The Basic Relationships

One possible approach is to expand the surplus on goods and services account to the point that it will completely offset the deficit on capital account. Such a scheme requires a reduction of imports with a less-than-offsetting reduction in exports or an increase in exports without a matching increase in imports.

Two basic forces dominate the net balance on current account: incomes and relative prices. Thus, the balance on current account can be enhanced by an increase in foreign prices, a decrease in U.S. prices, an increase in foreign income and stagnation in the United States G.N.P. It is probably but not necessarily true, that faster rates of growth abroad than in the United States and/or greater rates of price inflation abroad than in the United States will improve the U.S. balance on current account. However, any such advantage almost automatically brings with it negative feedback effects.

An increase in the United States surplus on current account can best be achieved by decreasing imports. The value of imports is very largely influenced by the level of prosperity enjoyed in the United States. Thus, any retardation of growth or failure to push the economy toward its full-employment potential G.N.P. will have the desired effect. There exists therefore a conflict between the domestic goal of full employment and the avoidance of the dollar deficit. To the extent that expansionary fiscal and monetary measures are foregone because of the dollar deficit, a cost has been incurred. In the same way, policies of restriction of aggregate demand can be instituted to restrain domestic price increases (so that foreign inflation will improve relative prices).

The Deficit

The deficit exists and has survived many measures, both temporary and semipermanent, which have been designed to help eradicate it. It has become a serious problem because it may induce a lack of faith in the U.S. dollar, which is an international medium of exchange and store of value vital to current international trade.

It is perhaps not so important that the deficit be eliminated as it is that it be shown to be capable of elimination. Unfortunately, the deficit has survived a sufficient number of policy measures that it can now only be shown to be capable of elimination by actually being eliminated for a respectable period. To achieve a balance in the international accounts will not be easy and good economic policy requires that this balance be achieved with minimum costs to both the American society and the world.

Three Principles[*]

My Lords, the experience of the years before the war has led most of us, though some of us late in the day, to certain firm conclusions. Three, in particular, are highly relevant to this discussion. We are determined that, in future, the external value of sterling shall conform to its internal value as set by our own domestic policies, and not the other way round. Secondly, we intend to retain control of our domestic rate of interest, so that we can keep it as low as suits our own purposes, without interference from the ebb and flow of international capital movements or flights of hot money. Thirdly, whilst we intend to prevent inflation at home, we shall not accept deflation at the dictate of influences from outside. In other words, we abjure the instruments of bank rate and credit contraction operating through the increase of unemployment as a means of forcing our domestic economy into line with external factors.

— JOHN MAYNARD KEYNES

[*] Address before the House of Lords on the International Monetary Fund, May 23, 1944, *The Parliamentary Debates* (Hansard), (London: H. M. Stationery Office, 1944), fifth series, vol. 131, p. 843.

PART ONE

MEASURES OF THE DEFICIT

INTRODUCTION

Some attention has already been devoted to the conceptual problems of measurement of the balance in international accounts. The problem of the "right" definition of a measure of imbalance—i.e., the definition which yields a summary indicator capable of serving as a basis for the appropriate policy decisions—can lead to arguments within a nation and to different solutions and methods of accounting among nations. The Federal Reserve Bank of St. Louis reviews three alternative measures proposed in the United States and two current foreign ones and applies these measures to the basic United States data. This exercise shows very clearly the variation in the size of the deficit which alternative systems of accounting can generate.

There is a real danger that a concept of the net balance which is biased toward a deficit may influence policy decisions toward restraint and the retardation of rates of growth. If this bias can be held by one nation, the bias can be held by all nations as a whole, with the result that all will institute international trade policies which tend to be more restrictive than is warranted and the world will, at least in the *ex ante* sense, enjoy a less than optimal volume of trade.[1]

The theory has been put forward that maintenance of a balance in international accounts imposes on an economy a discipline which is desirable in and of itself. This philosophy is nonrational in the sense that there is a confusion between the means and the ends. An economic philosophy should lay down certain economic goals for a society; the concept of an international balance should be viewed

---

[1] See Poul Høst-Madsen, "Asymmetries Between Balance of Payments Surpluses and Deficits," *I.M.F. Staff Papers* (July 1962), pp. 182–201.

as a constraint within which the goals must be achieved—a constraint which is somewhat analogous to the limitations imposed by the natural resource endowment—and should not be viewed as a goal for the attainment of which other ends may legitimately be sacrificed. Nor can a single goal (if balanced payments may conceivably be a legitimate goal) be considered apart from other goals when there is potentially substitution between them. This relationship is considered briefly by the authors of the Brookings Study below.

There is a second facet to the question of the discipline of the balance of international accounts which is understandably not covered by the Brookings authors. This is the question of correct policy in time of surplus. Clearly, the discipline of balance disappears in time of surplus and in these periods the arguments of those who propose severe restraint in times of deficit, assume an asymmetric character. The release of the constraint enjoins, or at least countenances, freedom for expansionary policies and an inflationary posture; but such policies do not characterize the philosophies of those who argue the intrinsic merit of constraint in periods of deficit. To such people inflation is abhorrent. Just as the optimal policy during periods of deficit can vary with the cause of the deficit, so too the optimal policy in periods of surplus can vary with the cause of the surplus. For example, a surplus caused by a domestic recession requires domestic expansion, if only because the acquisition of gold or other international assets is not a sufficient offset to the evils of unemployment through inadequate aggregate demand. If the correct counter for a surplus or deficit depends upon the cause of the imbalance and the situation in other nations, the achievement of balance cannot be a legitimate goal in itself and must be viewed as a means to an end.

Measurement of a Nation's Balance of Payments*

THERE has been unusual concern about the U. S. balance of payments since 1958. In recent years this account has been a vital consideration in the framing of both our domestic and our foreign economic policies. The state of our balance of payments has also affected the economic decisions of foreign governments and individuals.

Widespread attention has been focused on the nature of the balance of payments as an index of this country's international economic position. However, there are many ways of evaluating the balance of payments. A shorthand way is to select certain credit items (receipts) and certain debit items (payments) and to consider the difference between these payments and receipts as "surplus" or "deficit." The other debit and credit items can be considered as the means whereby the deficit or surplus is "settled" and the balance of payments "balanced." For example, in Table 1, under the "liquidity" approach to the balance of payments,[1] only the net change in our liquid liabilities to foreigners (including convertible foreign currency securities held by foreign monetary authorities) and net change in United States monetary reserve assets are the balancing items.

The size of a deficit depends upon which items are selected to measure it. To understand the significance of a deficit, it is important to realize the way in which it may be computed. This article outlines several alternative ways of measuring the balance-of-payments "deficit."

Two features of the present international payments system[2] — fixed exchange rates and the use of the dollar as an international

---

* From "Measurement of a Nation's Balance of Payments," *Federal Reserve Bank of St. Louis Review*, March 1964, pp. 6–10. Reprinted by permission of the Federal Reserve Bank of St. Louis.

[1] This measure has been perhaps the one most popular, or "traditional," in public discussion of the U.S. balance of payments. See the *Survey of Current Business*, December 1963, p. 11, Table 2, line C.1., for this measure.

[2] See this *Review*, July 1963, for a more complete discussion of the international payments system.

reserve currency — are especially relevant to the problem of evaluating the condition of the U. S. balance of payments. The United States as a member of the International Monetary Fund has agreed to maintain the value of its currency relative to gold. The authorities must stand ready to stabilize the value of the dollar in terms of other currencies. To do this, they need an adequate reserve of internationally acceptable non-dollar means of payment. Under present international monetary arrangements, the principal means of payment for this purpose are gold and convertible foreign currencies.

The extensive holding of dollar claims by other nations is an important consideration in evaluating the U. S. balance of payments. Since the dollar is one of the principal currencies used as a means of payment in world trade, foreigners hold dollar claims as working balances for financing trade. Dollar claims are also widely held by foreign countries as part of their international reserves. In large measure, foreigners are willing to hold dollar claims because the U. S. Treasury stands ready to convert dollars held by official foreign holders into gold upon demand. In order to determine the external liquidity position of the United States, therefore, it is necessary to take into account both its stock of international means of payment and the liquid dollar claims which are held by foreigners.

THE BALANCE-OF-PAYMENTS STATEMENT

A nation's balance of payments for a given period records the transactions between that nation and the rest of the world. As an accounting statement summarizing these transactions, and based on double-entry principles, the balance of payments always balances in the sense that debits always equal credits (Column I of Table I). However, even though a nation's balance of payments is continually in balance from an accounting viewpoint, the underlying economic relationships between that nation and others may be of an unsustainable character. It is in this latter sense that a "deficit" or "surplus" in the balance of payments may be a meaningful concept as part of an evaluation of the problems related to the balance of payments. In this sense, the implication is that market forces or policy measures will ultimately have to be brought to bear on the underlying character of the balance of payments if the external value of the nation's currency is to be maintained. To evaluate the balance of payments for any particular period — and thereby provide a guideline to policy steps — is thus a step in an analytical process.

CONCEPTS OF THE DEFICIT

Two of the most widely used approaches to balance-of-payments analysis are the "liquidity" approach and the "basic balance" approach.[3] A major purpose of analyzing the balance of payments is to appraise changes in the ability of a nation to maintain the external value of its currency in the face of potential and actual demands by holders of its currency for gold or other currencies. This ability will depend upon the state of the nation's external liquidity. For the United States, as a reserve currency country, the stock of internationally accepted means of payment relative to liquid claims held by foreigners against this stock define the state of external liquidity. For any given period, changes in external liquidity provide a measure of deficit or surplus in the balance of payments.

For other purposes, it is important for a nation to appraise its longer run competitive position, which is determined by underlying structural conditions in the world economy. In this basic approach, it is assumed that short-term flows of funds, which respond in large measure to relative interest rates and other short-run influences at home and abroad, are highly transitory. It is expected that these flows will largely reverse themselves in time, leaving the "basic balance" as the measure of deficit or surplus appropriate to evaluating the international performance of the economy.

THE LIQUIDITY APPROACH

The "overall" deficit in the balance of payments, measured according to the "liquidity" approach, is the sum of the decreases in liquid international assets and increases in liquid international liabilities (Column II, Table I). However, it is not a simple matter to determine which of our international resources and claims against them are "liquid" and thus relevant to the question of defending the gold convertibility of the dollar.

For the United States, liquid assets or resources are defined by the Department of Commerce to include gold, convertible foreign currencies held by U. S. authorities, and certain drawing rights on

[3] For a discussion of these various approaches to the balance of payments, see Hal B. Lary, *Problems of the United States as World Trader and Banker,* National Bureau of Economic Research, 1963; Walter S. Salant (and others), *The United States Balance of Payments in 1968,* Brookings Institution, 1963; Walther Lederer, *The Balance on Foreign Transactions: Problems of Definition and Measurement,* Princeton University, 1963.

TABLE I — UNITED STATES' BALANCE OF PAYMENTS, 1963*

[In billions of dollars]

Transactions	I Balance of Payments		II Overall (Liquidity)		III Regular		IV Basic	
	Receipts	Payments	Net Balance	Balancing Items	Net Balance	Balancing Items	Net Balance	Balancing Items
Merchandise Trade	21.7	16.9	+4.8		+4.8		+4.8	
Military Sales and Expenditures	0.8	2.9	−2.1		−2.1		−2.1	
Other Services	9.1	6.2	+2.9		+2.9		+2.9	
Remittances and Pensions		0.8	−0.8		−0.8		−0.8	
Government Grants and Capital	0.8	4.5	−3.7		−3.7		−3.7	
Private Long-term Capital	0.3	3.2	−2.9		−2.9		−2.9	
Private Short-term Capital	0.0	0.7	−0.7		−0.7			−0.7
Non-scheduled Receipts on Government Loans	0.3		+0.3			+0.3	+0.3	
Advances on Military Exports	0.2		+0.2			+0.2	+0.2	
Errors and Omissions		0.5	−0.5		−0.5			−0.5
Sales of Foreign Currency Securities	0.7			+0.7		+0.7		+0.7
Increase in Liquid Liabilities to Foreigners	1.5			+1.5		+1.5		+1.5
Decrease in U.S. Monetary Reserve Assets	0.4			+0.4		+0.4		+0.4
TOTAL	+35.8	−35.7	−2.5	+2.6	−3.0	+3.1	−1.3	+1.4

* Figures may not balance because of rounding.
Source: U.S. Department of Commerce.

the International Monetary Fund to which the United States has more or less automatic access.[4]

The types of liabilities included in liquid liabilities to foreigners are short-term liabilities to foreigners reported by U. S. banks and all foreign holdings of marketable U. S. Government securities.[5] Foreign holdings of certain nonmarketable U. S. Government securities, U. S. corporate and local government securities, and short-term liabilities to foreigners reported by nonfinancial U. S. concerns, are not considered to be liquid for this purpose.

The definitions of liquid resources and liabilities in the official U. S. balance-of-payments statistics have been criticized for being too conservative and hence overstating our deficit and the threat it poses

[4] The so-called "gold-tranche" position, which is equivalent to our quota less the Fund's holdings of dollars.

[5] Including nonmarketable, convertible foreign currency securities.

to defending the dollar. Private U. S. holdings of liquid claims abroad are not included as part of our international liquidity. These resources are excluded because (1) they are generally not readily available to U. S. authorities as a support for the dollar, and (2) the present statistical reporting practices do not permit a distinction between those private claims against foreigners that might be available to U. S. authorities from those that are not.

While claims of U. S. citizens against foreigners are excluded from the nation's stock of external liquidity, the country's liquid liabilities to foreigners include both official and private holdings. Aside from the problem of statistically separating official and private holdings, the rationale for this procedure is that although the U. S. Treasury need provide gold only to official holders of dollars, an attempt by foreign private holders to dispose of their dollar assets could result in an increase in official holdings of dollar claims. Also, foreign authorities generally can exercise effective control over private holdings of dollar claims. Therefore, private foreign holdings of liquid dollar assets constitute a potential demand on our liquid resources.

The practices followed in measuring the U. S. international liquidity position are not free from criticism. According to present methods of measurement, a movement of short-term dollar deposits to foreign banks by U. S. residents[6] would give rise to an increase in liquid liabilities to foreigners and an increase in the deficit (since the private U. S. dollar claim against the foreign bank is not included as a liquid asset in measuring the deficit). However, in view of the foreign bank's outstanding liability to the U. S. depositor, it cannot permanently dispose of the dollars for assets denominated in foreign assets.

Other illustrations of the measurement problem may be cited: when short-term funds are invested abroad to take advantage of higher interest rates, the U. S. investor may choose to protect himself against exchange risk by "hedging." That is, he may buy foreign currencies for present delivery and at the same time sell the currency for future delivery of dollars. By the U. S. liquidity criterion, the increased dollar liabilities to foreigners would increase the deficit, since the claim of U. S. investors for dollars to be delivered in the future is not considered a liquid asset in measuring the deficit.

Loans extended to foreigners by U. S. banks increase liquid claims against the United States and hence the deficit, according to

---

[6] See this *Review,* December 1963, for an exposition of the "Euro-dollar" market.

the liquidity measure. However, if foreigners are required to hold compensating balances in U. S. banks, then not all these dollar claims of foreigners represent a potential drain on our reserves. Another instance in which the deficit might be overstated is when "window dressing" (i.e., borrowings to improve balance sheet liquidity) operations of foreign commercial banks temporarily increase their dollar claims against the United States over the end of balance sheet periods. The U. S. deficit is thus overstated in one period, and then understated in the next period when the borrowings are repaid.

Aside from the criticism that the limitations of statistical reporting procedures may preclude a precise and appropriate measurement of net external liquid liabilities, there is the fundamental objection that any net external liquidity measure fails to provide an adequate measure of potential drain on our international reserves. Liquid liabilities to foreigners include those held by international organizations, foreign monetary authorities, and private foreigners. The motives for holding dollar claims vary considerably among these holders, and the potential drain on our reserves that these holdings represent is not the same for all holders. For example, that part of foreign dollar claims which constitute working balances for the finance of international trade is probably not as great a threat to liquidity position as those balances held for private investment purposes.[7]

More importantly, all liquid dollar assets, whether held by residents or foreigners, constitute a potential drain on our international liquidity as long as our residents may freely convert dollars to foreign currencies. In this sense, any liquidity approach overstates our capacity to defend the dollar.

THE BASIC BALANCE APPROACH

The deficit or surplus, viewed according to the basic balance approach, is the sum of the net transactions on goods and services, long-term capital movements, and government account (Column IV, Table I). This measure differs from the liquidity measure in that the net movements of short-term capital (including the "errors and omissions" item which is considered to be largely unrecorded short-term capital

---

[7] The emergence of various forms of central bank cooperation has been for the purpose of minimizing short-run speculative runs on the dollar and other currencies. To the extent that these arrangements are effective, the possibility of a "run on the dollar" is less likely.

flows) are regarded as a means of financing the deficit, rather than as part of the deficit. Thus, while a net outflow of U. S. short-term capital increases the "over-all" deficit, it has no effect on the "basic" deficit.

The rationale of this approach is that the transactions giving rise to the "basic" balance are considered to be "autonomous" whereas the other items are "accommodating." That is, trade in goods and services, long-term capital movements and government transactions are thought to be subject to longer run economic influences and political decisions. These "autonomous" items, which mainly reflect underlying competitive economic relationships, are the ones a country must balance if the external value of its currency is to be ultimately maintained.[8] The "accommodating" movements of private liquid funds are considered to be temporary, reflecting such factors as changing conditions in international money markets.

To the extent that it may be valid to make a distinction between these "autonomous" and "accommodating" transactions, the policy implications are clear. A nation should pursue those policies which will promote a reasonable basic balance over a longer period of time. Short-run policies which have their chief effect on short-term interest rates can quickly affect the accommodating transactions, but they will not directly redress the basic imbalance.

Unfortunately, in practice the forces affecting the basic balance are not clearly distinguishable from those affecting the accommodating transactions. Available evidence suggests that a major part of short-term capital movements are affected primarily by the level and pattern of international trade. It is also possible that basic transactions are to a significant extent affected by interest rates in the short run. For example, credit conditions may have a marked effect on inventory policy and hence imports.

Moreover, a reserve currency country such as the United States must consider the effect of short-term capital movements on the country's external liquidity position. While it is true that an increase in short-term investment abroad by U. S. residents gives rise to both a claim on and a liability to foreigners, for the period of the investment the foreign liability is a claim against the reserves of the United States. Because the dollar is a reserve currency, the aggregate volume of these claims could become a threat to our liquidity position.

[8] For the United States, it is possible that net short-term capital outflows might exist over time and be sustainable insofar as the additional foreign dollar claims which arise are held for purposes of international liquidity. In this case, a continuing basic deficit could exist.

OTHER MEASURES

Another widely used measure of the U. S. deficit is the "gross deficit" or balance on "regular" transactions (Column III, Table I).[9] This measure is equivalent to the "overall" balance (i.e., the "liquidity" measure) adjusted to exclude net receipts from "special" government transactions. Certain transactions between the United States and other governments — such as prepayment of foreign official debt to the United States, advances on military purchases from this country by foreign governments, and sales of certain types of U. S. Government nonmarketable securities to foreign governments — are undertaken *ad hoc* primarily as a means of improving the U. S. external liquidity position. These special transactions cannot be considered responsive to market forces or policy measures in the same sense as can "regular" transactions. Hence, the "regular" balance is a useful policy guideline indicating the magnitude of correction that is required in the balance of payments.

The chart on page 11 presents the U. S. balance-of-payments deficits for 1958–63, defined by "overall," "basic," and "regular" measures. Table I illustrates the computation of each of these deficit measures for the year 1963. The chart also shows what the U. S. deficit for 1958–63 would have been, using an approximation to the established practices of the United Kingdom and Japan. The U. K. measure is essentially similar to the basic balance outlined above, whereas the Japanese definition of surplus or deficit is a liquidity approach, comprising only changes in gross official holdings of gold and foreign currency assets. Table II shows what effect the use of alternative measures has on the magnitude of the U. S. deficit.

TABLE II — AVERAGE U.S. DEFICIT, 1958–1963 BY ALTERNATIVE MEASURES

[Billions of dollars]	
Overall	3.1
Basic	1.8
Regular	3.5
British Approach	2.1
Japanese Approach	1.1

Source: Basic data, U.S. Department of Commerce.

[9] See the *Survey of Current Business*, December 1963, p. 11, Table 1, line A.13.

ALTERNATIVE MEASURES OF THE U.S. BALANCE-OF-PAYMENTS DEFICIT

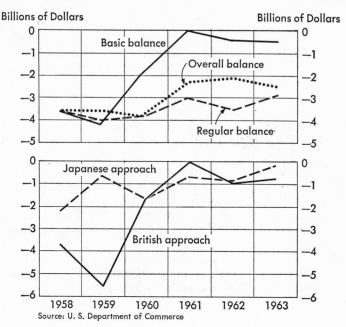

Source: U. S. Department of Commerce

SUMMARY

The U. S. balance-of-payments deficit has been presented under several alternative methods. No method is definitive. Institutional differences may justify different approaches. For the United States, a reserve currency country, it may be appropriate to focus upon its external liquidity position. In establishing economic policies to deal with a deficit, the "regular" balance may frequently be more meaningful for indicating the size of correction needed. On the other hand, if short-term capital flows tend to net out over time, then the basic balance provides a good long-run policy guideline.[10]

The approach employed by a country in measuring its balance of payments may have an impact on its national policies and may greatly affect its reactions to policies of other countries. For example, suppose that both the United States and the United Kingdom are

[10] *Cf.*, footnote 8, p. 9.

in balance-of-payments equilibrium. Suppose then that the British experience a deficit in their basic balance and that policy measures are taken to raise interest rates. If higher rates caused an inflow of short-term funds from the United States, it would be recorded as a U. S. deficit, using a "liquidity" measure. Everything else equal, the recorded U. S. deficit might be interpreted as requiring higher U. S. interest rates, and the effect of higher British rates attracting U. S. funds would be offset. If, on the other hand, the U. S. policy actions were guided by its "basic" balance, no remedial steps would be indicated. Thus, when different measures are used, the asymmetrical treatment of certain items can give rise to "surpluses" and "deficits" which might tend to serve as guidelines for conflicting national policies.

In conclusion, the measurement of a deficit is part of a larger analytical process in which the past is reviewed in order to shed light on a nation's international economic position. Many other factors must enter into the analysis — comparisons of national income levels, changes in costs and prices at home and abroad, conditions in international capital markets, and political decisions affecting government expenditures abroad. Public understanding may best be served by not attempting to evaluate the position of a nation in the world economy on the basis of one arbitrary figure.

WALTER S. SALANT AND ASSOCIATES

Basic Objectives and
the Balance of Payments*

FOUR national objectives that have high priority for the United States would be increasingly threatened by preoccupation with the balance of payments. These are:

* From Walter S. Salant et al., *The United States Balance of Payments in 1968* (Washington, D. C., 1963), pp. 243–245. Reprinted by permission of The Brookings Institution.

1. Achieving domestic economic stability and sustained growth at full employment.

2. Maintaining the military strength of the Free World.

3. Promoting and supporting economic development of underdeveloped areas and avoiding injury to the continued growth of other countries.

4. Assuring the greatest possible freedom of economically productive international transactions in the Free World.

It is often said that the maintenance of balance in international payments, if not an ultimate end of policy, is a means of restraining countries from pursuing undesirable economic policies. Balance-of-payments discipline, however, is desirable only as a means to ends; it is desirable only if the ends are desirable. If balance-of-payments considerations force a country to curb inflation or prevent misallocation of its real resources, the balance-of-payments discipline is a means toward a valid national objective, and is desirable. Such discipline is not desirable if it requires the subordination of higher-priority objectives. . . .

PART TWO

CAUSES OF THE DEFICIT

INTRODUCTION

So many component transactions make up the whole that any examination of the causation of the overall deficit must devote itself to a study of the sub-accounts. Each sub-account represents a possible contributory source of the deficit. This part surveys a whole range of possible causes for the deterioration of the current account and two different arguments on determination of that part of the capital account which makes the larger proportionate contribution to the overall deficit. The reader should remember, however, that because of the complex interrelationship no single component can be, so to speak, proven to be *the* source of the deficit. Rather the analyses should be read with a view to assessing alternative causes of the deficit as potential means of reducing the deficit in accordance with some specified criterion.

The two selections by Richard N. Cooper attempt to assess the competitiveness of the prices of the U.S. goods in foreign markets. The original was written in 1960 and is therefore somewhat dated, but it contains an excellent analysis of the causes underlying the relative decline in the U.S. balance on goods and services. The second article reappraises the situation some four years later. While Cooper is concerned predominantly with the overall competitiveness of manufacturing exports, John J. Arena examines the prices of consumer goods and his results tend to gainsay Cooper's optimism. The importance of noncommodity trade is briefly covered by Gray. Finally, the impact of the European Economic Community on the size of the deficit is analyzed by Lawrence B. Krause. These selections are oriented toward a review of factors affecting the magnitude of the United States surplus on current account.

The capital account is the immediate source of the deficit. However, it does not necessarily follow that if the deficit on capital account were removed, there would be no deficit in the U.S. accounts. The unknown quantity is the stimulus which the capital account deficit gives to the value of exports.

The deficit on capital account is incurred by both the private and government sectors. Capital exports by the private sector require little explanation as far as motive is concerned; capital flows in anticipation of a higher rate of return. Long-term private capital movements may be subdivided into direct and portfolio exports. Direct capital is employed in a productive venture under the control of American interests. To the extent that setting up or expanding productive capacity abroad requires the export of machinery, such capital exports are likely to have a relatively high, immediate feedback. On the other hand, portfolio capital usually seeks higher yields on stocks and bonds and offers no prospect of significant feedback. The distinction between the two types of private long-term capital exports is not as distinct as it might appear; for example, the decision of an American corporation to buy out foreign minority shareholders would be direct investment but would yield a feedback of the magnitude to be expected from portfolio investment.

Government long-term capital exports are strictly limited to long-term loans made net of repayments of earlier loans. In addition, the government account includes foreign aid in its many various forms. *A priori,* it is to be expected that loans and grants of this type will be very quickly disbursed by the recipients. The feedback therefore should be quite high. However, it does not necessarily follow (except in the case of the sale of agricultural surplus) that the disbursement will necessarily enhance American commodity and service exports— although more careful scrutiny of loan and aid applications may recently have raised the proportionate feedback.

The statement of the Hon. David E. Bell, Administrator, Agency for International Development, reviews the relation between foreign aid and the deficit. N. R. Danielian and his associates disregard the whole question of feedback in their remarks on the governmental responsibility for the deficit. Their conclusions and recommendations suffer from the same tendency to ignore feedback from government expenditures, but at the same time tend to stress the feedback from

private capital exports. Similarly, they tend to disregard the delay
between the direct capital export and the return flow of interest and
dividends. However, the statement is both searching and provocative
and contains many suggestions for curbing the deficit which merit
further investigation and study.

RICHARD N. COOPER

The Competitive Position
of the United States*

THE NEWLY aroused concern about the competitive position of
the United States in world trade is a measure of the impact of three
years of a balance-of-payments deficit of $3–$4 billion a year. The
deficit is attributable to a number of factors, some of them having
nothing to do with the ability of American business to compete in
world markets. But the startling rise in imports in 1958 and 1959 —
e.g., the prevalence of German, Japanese, Dutch, English, and
Italian products among the average child's Christmas gifts — brought
the balance-of-payments problem home to the common man and
jarred a complacent public into raising questions about America's
ability to carry its enormous self-imposed financial commitments
abroad.

Yet during these same three years the merchandise exports of
the United States exceeded its imports by more than $3 billion a year
on the average. This is not the mark of a country with a weak
competitive position. The following pages attempt to clarify what is
meant by a country's "competitive position," to view some of the
evidence suggesting that the competitive position of the United States
may have weakened in recent years, and to examine some of the

* An abridgement of Richard N. Cooper's "The Competitive Position of the
United States" in *The Dollar Crisis* edited by Seymour E. Harris, © 1961 by
Harcourt, Brace & World, Inc. and reprinted with their permission.

explanations which have been put forward in connection with this alleged deterioration.

THE MEANING OF "COMPETITIVE POSITION"

It is worth noting at the outset that in classical trade theory's world of barter it is meaningless to ask whether a country's competitive position is strong or weak. Every import has its counterpart in an export. To be sure, some countries excel in the cheap production of certain goods; but they are relatively inefficient in the production of others. It is *relative* costs, not the absolute level of costs, which determine the pattern of trade. Under competition, that country which can produce a good at the least relative cost finds itself producing the good with a surplus just sufficient to exchange for meeting its deficiencies in relatively high-cost goods.

This is the traditional theory of comparative advantage. But the theory is several stages removed from reality, and as it relates to the modern world it is best thought of merely as an "existence theorem": no matter what the resource endowments, the productive capacities, and the pattern of demand in a country, some rate of exchange *exists* between its currency and others which will induce it to trade with other countries and will allow it to do so continuously without jeopardizing its international reserves.[1] This exchange rate is not necessarily the one prevailing at the present time; nor does the theorem postulate automatic forces which lead us to it. But at least it assures us that any country, whether by chance or by careful analysis, can at each point in time find an exchange rate between its currency and others which will allow it to compete effectively in world markets with neither deficit nor surplus.

In keeping with the classical view, the competitive position of a country, as used here, will refer to its *trade* position. A country can run continuing and even rising trade surpluses and still lose gold and foreign exchange due to unfavorable movements in the other items of the total balance of payments. Thus a country's trade is only one item — albeit usually the largest one — out of many influencing the country's foreign asset position and affecting confidence in its currency. Interest frequently focuses on trade — imports and exports of goods and services — because it is felt that trade is somehow more

[1] The technician will note an exception to this general rule: If the pattern of relative costs is identical between the country and the rest of the world, trade between them will not be beneficial. Furthermore, changes in demand or production technique might require movement to a different exchange rate.

"basic" than the other international receipts and payments, and hence reflects more accurately the "underlying" or "true" position of a country, while other movements represent mere surface phenomena compared with it.

This is by no means the case. While it is true that many foreign payments are essentially transitory and will either cease or reverse themselves in a short time, others are as permanently a part of the balance of payments as is the import bill. These items — long-term investment abroad, government expenditures abroad for mutual security, payments of interest on foreign investment, payments to pensioners living abroad, and so on — represent together what can be called the country's foreign "commitments." A surplus in the balance of payments requires that the net payments for these items be over-balanced by net receipts in the exchange of goods and services.[2] It is therefore possible for a country to have a competitive position which is very strong, but not "strong enough" to cover its foreign commitments.

It is not easy to find a single, widely accepted measure of the competitive strength of a country in world markets. One appropriate measure for this would seem to be the ratio of its export surplus to its total exports,[3] a measure which indicates the relative amount of export receipts which are available for uses other than paying for imports. The larger the foreign commitments of the country, the larger must be its export surplus if its total payments are to remain in balance. It was the function of the classical mechanism of adjustment in international trade to assure that just that degree of competitiveness would be achieved which was required to meet the country's foreign commitments.

HAS THE COMPETITIVE POSITION OF THE UNITED STATES DECLINED?

A Look at the Record

It must be remembered that in 1958, and again in 1960, the excess of exports over imports of the United States was greater than that of any peacetime year before 1956 except for 1951 and the years imme-diately following World War I and World War II, when American

---

[2] I have not followed the usual practice of including interest on foreign invest-ment as payment for a "service."

[3] More appropriately, in a free enterprise economy, the ratio of commercial export surplus to all commercial exports. But in practice it is difficult to separate "noncommercial" exports and imports from United States trade returns.

exports were considerably inflated by reconstruction aid to Europe. This fact must temper any discussion of the United States competitive position.

Table I sets out the export ratio for recent years and for selected years in the past. It can be seen that, except for 1959, the export ratio was about the same in the past few years as it was in the first half of the 1950's, but was very much lower than the ratios in 1956 and 1957, when American exports were lifted first by a vigorous investment boom in Europe, then by the extraordinary fuel demands following the closing of the Suez Canal in late 1956.

TABLE I — TRADE AND FOREIGN COMMITMENTS

	1896–1914 (annual average)	1928	1937
1. Exports of goods and services a	$ 1.70	$ 5.76	$ 3.98
2. Imports of goods and services b	1.44	5.15	3.92
3. Balance (1–2)	.25	.62	.06
4. Foreign commitments c	.26	.40	−.53
5. Export ratio (3÷1)	15.0	10.7	1.4
6. Ratio of commitments to exports (4÷1)	15.3	6.9	−13.3

a Excluding income from foreign investment and shipments under military grant.

b Excluding United States military expenditures abroad and interest and dividend payments on foreign investment in the United States.

c Net long-term investment abroad (less earnings), military expenditures abroad, net long-term foreign investments in the United States (less earnings), and unilateral transfers (except grants of military equipment).

1951–55 (annual average)	1956	1957	1958	1959	1960 e
[In billions of dollars]					
$16.34	$20.86	$23.60	$20.28	$20.42	$23.52
13.65	16.28	16.93	16.86	19.64	19.71
2.69	4.58	6.66	3.42	.78	3.80
4.14	5.73	6.70	6.97	5.30 d	6.00
[In percentages]					
16.5	21.9	28.2	16.9	3.8	16.2
25.3	27.5	28.4	34.5	25.9	25.5

d Excluding the increase in the United States quota at the International Monetary Fund.

e The first three quarters at an annual rate.

Source: U.S. Department of Commerce, *Survey of Current Business*, various issues.

Despite this decline in the past few years, the export ratio is still quite respectable by all historical standards. At the same time, however, American commitments abroad, far from declining, have increased enormously as American responsibility for world leadership has increased. Payments for these commitments, comprising troop expenditure abroad, grants and loans for development, private investment abroad by American firms and individuals, and the like, now amount to about a third of the total payments for imports, and equaled over a quarter of the export receipts in 1960. The export ratio must grow as foreign commitments grow, relative to total exports, as indeed it has done, though not sufficiently.

Superficially, an objection can be raised to the export ratio as a measure of competitiveness: over the short run it will vary not only with variation in relative costs and prices among countries; it will also vary with the state of foreign demand, rising if the world economy outside the United States is booming, falling when it slumps. Similarly, the export ratio will vary with the American business cycle to the extent that the latter is out of phase with business demand abroad. As usually used, "competitiveness" refers to the underlying cost conditions, either among firms or among countries. It is somewhat misleading, however, to attempt to exclude demand considerations from a discussion of competitiveness in foreign trade. While it may be useful to separate demand factors from supply considerations when analyzing a closed economy, any such neat distinction in questions of foreign trade is liable to obscure the fact that demand for foreign products depends intimately on both domestic demand and domestic supply. Demand for imports is likely to increase during the upward phase of a country's business cycle because demand for most products is rising. But the same boom also restricts the supply of goods available for export.

Export Shares

Change in a country's share in total world exports is a commonly used measure of change in competitiveness. It is mistakenly thought that the use of shares eliminates the influence of demand factors, since exports are "deflated" by total world exports, thereby supposedly isolating the changes in a country's position which are due to changes in relative prices and other supply factors. Once again, however, if fluctuations in business activity from country to country are out of phase, export shares will reflect these same demand factors in much the same way that the export ratio will. A decline in a country's export share indicates that its exports are growing less rapidly (or are falling more rapidly) than the exports of all other countries taken together. This circumstance might be due to relative price changes in its disfavor; but for a country as large as the United States it might also be due to its *imports* having grown more rapidly than world imports, as in the vigorous phase of a business cycle. Imports of the United States necessarily constitute part of the total exports of other countries; so if they fall, the United States share of exports will automatically rise. In 1960 the respectable United States export share was undoubtedly due in part to booming conditions abroad combined with considerable slack in the United States.

The size of the share, of course, depends upon the size of the country and its need to trade; but movements in the share suggest how its competitive position may be changing.

TABLE II — UNITED STATES SHARE OF TOTAL WORLD EXPORTS AND EXPORTS OF MANUFACTURES (IN PER CENT)

	United States share of total world exports [a]	United States share of world exports of manufactures [a]
1913	12.7	9.7
1926–29	15.8	16.3
1938	14.0	21.7
1950	17.7	27.3
1952	18.4	26.2
1954	17.0	25.1
1956	18.7	25.3
1958	17.2	23.3
1960 [b]	17.4	21.8

a Excluding United States shipments under military grant from both United States and world totals.
b First half.

Sources: League of Nations, *Industrialization and Foreign Trade*, 1945; and United Kingdom Board of Trade, *Report on Overseas Trade*, November 1960.

Table II shows the United States share of total world exports and of world exports of manufactures. It can be seen that the United States' share of the total is considerably higher than it was before World War II, commensurate with the great rise in American commitments abroad, but that since that time there has been no substantial change. In contrast, the United States' share of world exports of manufactures, which account for about two-thirds of all American exports, has fallen considerably during the past decade. Moreover, maintenance of the total export share is due in considerable measure to shipments abroad of agricultural products under Public Law 480, whereby certain commodities can be "sold" for nonconvertible currencies which are then for the most part lent to the importing governments. Such shipments have risen sharply since the program was started in 1954 and now account for just under one-third of all United States agricultural exports.

Overall share data suffer from the defect of any aggregate figures; they obscure compositional changes. It is theoretically possible, for example, for the United States export share to have *risen* for each product in every market, yet for the total export share to have *fallen*. This bizarre result would occur if the markets in which the United States share was relatively low had increased their imports rapidly compared with the markets in which the United States had a substantial share.

Taking this possibility into account, the Department of Commerce did a thorough study on United States export shares of manufactured goods.[4] The study compares actual United States exports of forty-five important commodity groups to six regional markets in 1958 to a hypothetical export total computed on the assumption that its share in each of the resulting 270 commodity-area markets was the same in 1958 as was its average share for the period 1954–56. For example, in computing the hypothetical exports of iron and steel products to Latin America the United States was assumed to have had in 1958 the same share of total world exports of iron and steel products to Latin America as it had had in 1954–56. An interesting discovery of this procedure is that these detailed American export shares did not change so much as the decline in the share of all manufactured exports would suggest. Rather, total imports into Canada and Latin America, two areas in which the American share is relatively high, slumped more than imports into areas in which the United States share is low. This relative stagnation of markets traditionally preferring American goods accounted for about 40 per cent of the decline in the total American export share. Moreover, the study observes that exports of three commodity groups — trucks and automobiles, iron and steel products, and commercial aircraft — accounted for 96 per cent of the remainder of the decline.

A similar analysis for 1959 reveals that the decline in market shares was somewhat more widespread than in 1958, although again three commodity groups alone accounted for three-fourths of the decline. If the United States had maintained the export shares which

---

[4] United States Department of Commerce, "Analysis of Changes in U.S. Shares of Export Markets for Manufactures, 1954–1958."

prevailed in 1954–56, American exports of manufactures in 1959 would have been nearly a billion dollars greater than the $9 billion that they were.

To sum up, while evidence for the view that there has been a recent decline in American competitive ability in world markets is far from overwhelming, some evidence does point in that direction. The United States export ratio has averaged somewhat less in the last three years than it averaged in the earlier part of the decade; and while the American share of world exports has been roughly maintained, this has been due partly to noncommercial transactions. The export share of manufactured products has fallen noticeably, even after correcting for shifts in market composition. Furthermore, the years 1958–60 were not notable for a high level of economic activity in the United States. While it is true that the gross national product finally reached the enormous sum of half a trillion dollars, it did so at a limping pace. Unemployment averaged 5.2 per cent during this period. If domestic economic activity had been more vigorous, imports of raw materials and semifabricated products would have been considerably higher, making the trade position still less favorable than it was.

Other evidence pointing toward a decline in American competitiveness can be found. For example, the proportion of total World Bank loans spent in the United States has fallen without interruption, from an excessively high average of 63 per cent up to mid-1955, to only 29 per cent in the fiscal year 1960. The normal procedure for spending these loans, in the words of the Fifteenth Annual Report of the Bank, "is for borrowers to place their orders on the basis of international competition." The greater part of this American loss in export shares of World Bank purchases in the past four years was captured by the United Kingdom, Italy, and Japan.

Evidence of slippage also appears in American imports, which rose from 5.3 per cent of all movable goods produced in the United States in 1953 to 6.1 per cent in 1959. Even in 1960, a year in which total imports declined slightly from the high of 1959, imports of manufactured products kept pace with the 5 per cent rise in disposable income. And the number of firms which have parts manufactured abroad is growing.

There has been no wholesale retreat in foreign and domestic markets by American producers; the decline in most shares has been gradual and partially offset by rises in others. Indeed, some economists do not accept as a fact a deterioration in the competitive position of the United States. But the evidence adduced above lends some support to those who do, and it is time to turn to several of the explanations for the gradual worsening of the United States position in world markets.

EXPLANATIONS FOR THE DECLINE IN COMPETITIVENESS

Of the explanations for the recent deterioration, four stand out as meriting close attention. The first, popular with the press and with some members of the banking community, is that inflation in the United States has continued so persistently that the country has "priced itself out of the world markets." Whatever favorable competitive position the United States may have had in the past, this view holds that it has been dissipated by the intransigent rise in prices which has occurred since 1956. Only the combined effects of an investment boom in Europe and the trade disruptions of the Suez crisis delayed its effects on American trade. Whatever is the cause of inflation, inflation is the cause of the deficit; and as long as domestic inflation persists there will be trouble with the trade balance.

A second explanation considers price changes relatively unimportant in determining the level and composition of American trade, but argues that the United States, traditionally vigorous in designing new products, has lost some of its pre-eminence as the most advanced country in production technique, product design, and innovation.

A third explanation focuses attention not on recent price changes but on the low level of prices, in terms of dollars, with which the devaluations of 1949 left many of America's competitors. These low prices, combined with an extraordinary rise in the productive capacity required for meeting demand at these prices, have resulted finally in a spectacular rise in the exports of such countries as Germany, Italy, Japan, and the Netherlands. In other words, recent events merely reflect long-standing patterns in comparative advantage.

A final line of reasoning attributes the recent change in the American competitive position to "structural" changes in demand or supply rather than to general price inflation.

We will consider each of these explanations, in reverse order.

Structural Change

One popular version is that the striking fall in the trade surplus in 1958 and 1959 resulted from a series of "special commodity problems." The trouble can be laid on cotton, coal, iron and steel, automobiles, aircraft, and a few other select groups. The Department of Commerce study mentioned earlier inclines toward this view. If American producers had designed smaller cars sooner, if Britain had not gained a lead in the production of commercial jet aircraft, if the Department of Agriculture had been more sensitive to market forces in pricing its cotton for export, if the steel strike had not lasted for six months — then the United States trade position would have been stronger. Recall that cars and trucks, iron and steel mill products, and commercial aircraft accounted in 1958 for over 96 per cent of the amount by which exports of manufactures fell short of the hypothetical value of exports based on 1954–56 shares. These three groups accounted for 78 per cent of the difference in 1959. Cotton exports in 1959 were 38 per cent lower than in 1956, and coal exports were 48 per cent lower. But now the unrealistic pricing policy in cotton has been corrected, American automobile manufacturers have produced their "compacts," and American commercial jets are finally flowing into international trade. Coal is likely to be depressed as long as European countries maintain import quotas in the face of their own large surpluses; and iron and steel products seem to present special problems. But generally these "special commodity problems" are viewed as temporary and self-correcting; deficits of the past few years according to this view should be regarded as the coincidence of several short-lived misfortunes indicative of nothing in particular for the future.

C. P. Kindleberger has suggested that structural changes go beyond the mere "special commodity problem." In the past few years Americans have lifted "the horizon of [their] economic vision more completely to the world level." Americans are now more willing to accept — indeed to prefer — both foreign merchandise and foreign securities. A decade of foreign travel and living abroad, of foreign export drives in the United States, and of a steady flow of information in the press about foreign goods and foreign peoples has increased American interest in and knowledge about foreign products.

This applies to American producers as well as consumers. Increasingly American firms have become *aware* of the possibility of manufacturing parts abroad, for example. It is not merely the relative decline of foreign prices, nor the easing of their production position, but the increasing American awareness of these things which has brought about the change.

While there is undoubtedly a good deal of truth to all this, one might well ask why Americans did not notice also tremendous possibilities for export abroad. Or do these not exist? Moreover, while it is probably true that consumer acceptance of foreign cars has increased over the years, is it entirely an accident that the ownership of foreign cars is highest in those areas of the country where income is highest? In a growing economy it is difficult to separate "structural" changes in taste from changes in the pattern of demand resulting from rising incomes. With a trebling of the number of families owning two or more cars in the past decade, the rise in demand for small, economical foreign cars, especially suited to urban living, becomes less of a mystery.

An analytical difficulty also rests with the "special commodity problem" explanation for structural change. In some cases it is possible to point to highly specific, easily identifiable reasons for a great decline in exports. The European import quotas on coal would be an example. But this is not always possible, and the fact that several commodity groups account for the bulk of the change is not sufficient evidence to deny a general cause for the decline. Broad forces frequently exert more pressure on some items than on others — just as a drop of 10 per cent in an individual's income is more likely to cause great changes in his expenditure on some goods and little or no change on others than it is to cause a uniform reduction in his expenditure on all goods.

This is not to deny that there may have been some special factors in recent trade developments — what would imports of foreign cars have been if Ford had decided in 1955 to produce the Falcon rather than the Edsel? Where human decisions are continually involved in producing and pricing new products in markets endemic with uncertainty, mistakes are bound to be made which can only be corrected in time. But explanation can occur at a variety of levels; seemingly special and highly individual factors may manifest more general forces at work, and explanations tailored to fit each occurrence should not be allowed to obscure these forces.

Three such forces bearing on United States trade can be mentioned. They are the growth of European capacity, the gradual decline in American technological and production lead, and inflation in the United States.

The Growth of Foreign Capacity

Several economists have argued that the recent turn in the country's trade position attests to the success of American reconstruction aid to Europe and Japan. Rebuilt from the destruction of war, productive capacity in some countries is rarely more than ten years old. Not only are productive facilities modern, but they have been increased at a rapid rate. Industrial production between 1953 and 1960 grew

76 per cent in the seventeen OEEC countries (and 168 per cent in Japan), compared with only 20 per cent in the United States. Thus the ability of foreign manufacturers to satisfy new orders for goods has increased enormously in the past ten years.

This great rise in capacity, coupled with a generally low level of costs, is seen as one cause for pressure on the United States trade position. Most foreign countries gained a great price advantage relative to the United States when, led by the pound sterling in 1949, major currencies were devalued up to 30.5 per cent. While some of this price advantage was necessary to re-align the world's economies to the new conditions of the postwar world (for example, Britain's large loss in income from overseas investments), there is a general consensus that the devaluations went further than was required. A part of the foreign price advantage was dissipated in the inflation accompanying the Korean War, but foreign prices in terms of dollars remained well below their predevaluation levels. In terms of dollars, between 1938 and 1955 the price level of the gross national product for the OEEC countries combined rose only 78 per cent as much as the United States level rose.[5]

Most authorities agree that the postwar recovery had generally been completed by 1953. What delayed the assault of low foreign prices and large capacity on the United States trade position?

The most obvious answer is that vigorous demand conditions, especially in Europe, have limited the incentives of foreign producers to export. The European boom in 1956 followed by the 1957 aftermath of the Suez crisis may have obscured trends which began earlier. Finally, the mass organization and distributive system required for marketing in the United States cannot be built overnight. A process started in 1950 may only recently have begun to bear fruit.

The Loss in Technical Lead and Product Innovation

Some authorities have suggested that in a dynamic world the law of comparative advantage offers little guide to the analyst, for the structure of comparative advantage is continually changing. The United States, in particular, was cast in the role of the scientist-inventor who, while perhaps really an inefficient producer, was constantly developing new products which either put his suppliers out of business or stimulated their desires. In manufacturing, the "research-orientation"

[5] OEEC, *Statistics on Sources and Uses of Finance,* 1948–58, 1960, p. 23. Several British economists have argued the same point from a different angle.

of its products is supposed to be one of America's greatest advantages. As long as they could keep ahead of their foreign counterparts in the development of new products, American producers did not need to scrutinize too carefully their relative cost position.

This research lead may be declining. Not long after transistors became a commercial product, the Japanese were exporting pocket-sized radios on a vast scale (although American producers seem to be regaining the lead by developing an efficient transistor-making machine). The two-year lag behind the British in delivery of commercial jet airliners is another example. And one need only look around a toy shop to observe the considerably greater taste and imagination demonstrated by the foreign products.

Furthermore, the remarkable increase in recent years in the use of licensing agreements may shorten still further the technological lead of the United States.

Priced out of World Markets?

The most popular explanation for the recent deterioration of the United States trade position is that continuing domestic inflation is pricing American producers out of world markets. Indeed there has been a considerable rise in prices in the United States, first from the outbreak of the Korean War until mid-1952, then recommencing in late 1956. The latter rise, especially, is depicted as having boosted United States price levels just enough to overcome consumer inertia and induce a shift to foreign products. The appearance of low-priced consumer products on the market, combined with increasing reports from manufacturers that they are turning abroad for parts and semi-fabricated products, seems to confirm this view. American bicycle factories are now alleged to be little more than assembly points for foreign parts. The very large increase since 1956 in United States direct investment abroad is sometimes attributed to the same cause.

Any of the previous hypotheses mentioned could explain the same observations: a "broadening of horizons" could account for foreign parts purchases as well as higher domestic prices could. So could increased foreign capacity at (existing) low prices. Furthermore, it is too often forgotten that foreign trade depends upon relative prices, not upon the absolute level in one country alone. While the United States has experienced a substantial rise in prices since 1956, so have many other countries. Inflation has been a world-wide phenomenon. Table III compares some of the measures of inflation for the United States and several of its important competitors.

TABLE III — MEASURES OF PRICE MOVEMENT (1953=100)

	Consumer price index	Price index of GNP	Hourly earnings in manufacturing
	1959	*1958*	*1959*
Belgium	110	112	133
France b	92	104	113
West Germany	112	113	148
Italy	113	110	127
Netherlands	119	120	143
Sweden	120	117	134
United Kingdom	120	120	142
OEEC combined		115	
Canada	110	113	126
Japan	110	107	136 e
United States	109	112	135

Sources: OEEC, *General Statistics* and *Statistics of Sources and Uses of Finance;* United Nations *Monthly Bulletin of Statistics* and *Current Economic Indicators,* various issues.

Wholesale price index of finished goods				Unit value of exports			
1957	1958	1959	1960 a	1957	1958	1959	1960 a
n.a. c	n.a.	n.a.	n.a.	106	99	95	n.a.
99	94	86	89	99	97	90	93
106 d	107 d	107 d	107 d	103	103	100	101
106 d	102 d	100 d	101 d	95	91	83	88
107	105	105	105	107	101	98	99
109	109	109	111	106	101	99	101
110	111	112	112	110	109	108	110
				105	102	99	100
104	104	106	106	103	102	104	104
102 d	99 d	100 d	99 d	97	94	95	98
107	109	109	110	107	106	107	108

a First half.
b In United States dollars.
c Not available.
d Producers' goods.
e Monthly earnings.

It is clear from the data that, however severe inflation may have been in the United States, it was perhaps even more pronounced abroad. The consumer price index went up less since 1953 in the United States than in any other country listed except France, where the low value is attributable to currency devaluations in mid-1957 and at the end of 1958. The price index of the gross national product — perhaps the most comprehensive measure of price movements — also rose less in the United States than in most other countries, rising 12 per cent from 1953 to 1958 compared with 13 per cent in

Germany, 20 per cent in the United Kingdom, and 15 per cent in the seventeen Western European countries combined.

Because so much emphasis is placed on high and rising American wages, it is worth noting that hourly earnings in manufacturing grew only 25 per cent between 1953 and 1959 in the United States, substantially less than the 36 per cent rise in Japan, the 42 per cent rise in the United Kingdom, and the 48 per cent rise in Germany. Once again, only the rise in France (in dollars) fell short of that in the United States. It must be remarked, however, that a 1 per cent rise in the high American wage is considerably larger in absolute terms than a 1 per cent rise in the low wages of Japan or even Germany.

These figures seem to scotch the argument that general inflation in the United States has caused a decline in competitiveness. Several measures give the same result. However, each of these indicators is defective for the purpose of examining the effects on trade. The consumer price index fails to include the prices of producer goods, which are very important in trade but have only an indirect effect

FIGURE I. EXPORTS OF MANUFACTURES, 1959 (1953 = 100)

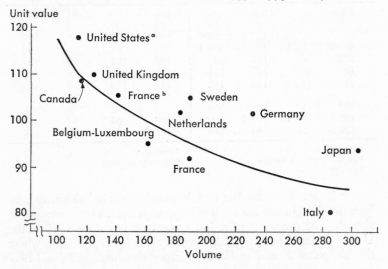

[a] Excluding shipments under military grant.
[b] 1958.

Sources: United Nations Statistical Office, *Yearbook of International Trade Statistics*; and Sir Donald MacDougall, *The Dollar Problem: A Reappraisal*, 1960, p. 19.

on the price of consumer goods. While the "cost-of-living" index may have an important effect on foreign travel — and on the temptations for the pensioner to live abroad — it fails as an indicator of price movements in traded goods. The GNP deflator includes the prices of all goods, but also includes prices of many items which cannot enter foreign trade at all. Services comprise a large and growing part of the total output of most economies — over 35 per cent in the United States — and are notorious for their rapidly rising prices. And wage changes alone are an imperfect guide in that they take account neither of nonwage costs of production nor of changes in labor productivity. The manufacturer is less interested in the cost of an *hour* of labor than in the cost of the *product* of labor.

Wholesale price indices are weighted too heavily with standard, uniform goods to be truly representative of any country's "bundle" of exports, but on this measure the United States shows up less well, demonstrating a larger rise since 1953 than any other country except the United Kingdom. The same is true for the unit value of exports, a comprehensive (though not exceedingly good) measure of the price of export goods. In fact, as Figure I shows, there is a noticeable relationship between export unit values and the volume of exports of manufactures. It is possible to perceive a downward-sloping demand curve for exports of manufactures (which for the reader's benefit has been sketched in), though the relationship is quite loose.[6] Germany and Japan did considerably better than one would have expected on the basis of price movements alone (keeping in mind that the chart shows only *changes* in unit values, not the relative *levels*), perhaps lending some credence to the "excessive devaluation *cum* growth in capacity" argument. France and Belgium did less well than one might have expected on the basis of relative price movements, although in the case of France the end-of-1958 devaluation may have been too close to allow full impact on its exports of manufactures in 1959. France has also been plotted for 1958.

[6] This is not the static demand curve of microeconomic theory. World demand for exports of manufactures has been growing throughout the period. The curve reflects this growth in total demand and suggests that those countries with little increase in export prices captured more than their share of this rise in demand. It should be kept in mind, too, that a rise in the price of certain key commodities can have repercussions throughout the entire wholesale (or export) price index. Otto Eckstein and Gary Fromm have estimated the indirect effects of the rise in steel prices on the wholesale price index in their "Steel and the Postwar Inflation," Study Paper No. 2, *Study of Employment, Growth, and Price Levels,* Joint Economic Committee, 1959.

An Alternative View: Short-Run and Long-Run Factors

It appears that the general measures of price change obscure inflationary tendencies which have in fact placed some American products at a competitive disadvantage. A recent analysis of inflation in the United States has argued that the 1956–59 rise in prices was fundamentally "demand-pull" in nature, even though there seemed to be no excess aggregate demand.[7] The explanation of this apparent paradox lies in an asymmetry in price behavior between economic sectors under heavy demand pressure and sectors in which demand is slack. As the pattern of demand shifts in favor of certain products, prices in those sectors rise. But because of institutional rigidities prices fail to fall in those sectors *from* which demand has shifted. Thus a combination of demand shifts and great resistance to downward movement in industrial prices results in an upward movement of any general price index. This is the so-called sectoral demand inflation.

As it happens, it is precisely those sectors which benefited from a rise in demand which participate heavily in American exports: non-electrical machinery, transport equipment, metals, and metal manufactures. While exports of these items naturally suffered, the absence of price reductions failed to stimulate export demand for other products to an offsetting degree. The European countries, in contrast, suffered no such imbalance in price rises.

This difference in behavior itself deserves an explanation. Recorded foreign prices appear more flexible than American prices, as a glance at the last eight columns of Table III suggests. When international demand slackened in 1958, foreign export prices fell somewhat more than American prices. As the European boom commenced, export unit values began to rise. A part of this cyclical behavior in foreign export prices may be explained by the higher share of raw-material costs in total manufacturing costs abroad.[8] As raw-material prices fall there is a proportionally greater reduction in foreign production costs than in American costs. Secondly, raw-material prices, determined in world commodity markets, are generally more flexible abroad. For example, copper prices in the United States are notoriously rigid compared with those determined at the London Metal Exchange. British mills have indicated a decided preference for the more flexible prices. Both factors make possible a

[7] C. L. Schultze, "Recent Inflation in the United States," Study Paper No. 1, *Study of Employment, Growth, and Price Levels*, Joint Economic Committee, 1959.

[8] Theodore R. Gates, "Production Costs Here and Abroad," *Studies in Business Economics*, No. 61, National Industrial Conference Board, 1958.

greater reduction in product prices where cost reductions are passed on to the buyer.

By no means the whole of European and Japanese price inflexibility can be explained in this way. Raw-material prices were still low in 1960, yet foreign export unit values began to rise again. This behavior suggests that foreign business is readier than American business, to trim prices in periods of excess capacity. Oriented primarily toward a large domestic market and operating increasingly in a milieu in which price reductions do not occur, American business is perhaps reluctant to jeopardize delicate domestic price relationships by lowering prices to sell competitively on a world market — a version of the "rachet effect" mentioned so frequently in the current literature on inflation. Foreign businessmen on the average do a much higher proportion of their business in international trade, and they may rely much more on foreign sales to absorb any excess capacity produced by slack in domestic demand. If this hypothesis is correct, recovery from recession in the United States and abroad should bring a reversal of these price relationships.

If this is an accurate and full statement of the situation, the recent decline in American competitiveness is merely a temporary phenomenon and will not recur until the next pause in the economic growth of the European and Japanese economies. A cyclical decline in competitive position can be expected to be offset by a cyclical rise whenever these economies boom, leading to shortages and price increases abroad. It is worth noting that three-fourths of the substantial rise in American exports in 1960 went to Western Europe and Japan, both areas having experienced a sharp upturn in economic activity. And as foreign exchange earnings rise elsewhere in the world, the price increases and supply shortages which Europe is now experiencing should redound to the benefit of American exports.

This optimistic appraisal is marred somewhat by an examination of wage costs. While, as we have seen, wage costs per hour have risen rather less in the United States than in some competing countries, hourly output has also risen less. In several countries wage costs per unit of output have even declined since the early fifties. Other countries, to be sure, have fared worse than the United States in this repect, but the steady upward march in unit labor costs does represent a persistent drag on American sales abroad.

SUMMARY AND PROSPECTS

The competitive trade position which a country must attain depends upon its international financial commitments, and any assessment of its competitive position in world markets must be set against these commitments. The United States today has financial obligations abroad greater than at any other period in its peacetime history. Some of these obligations are self-imposed, some are imposed by world tensions and the force of events. Not only does the United States, as a nation, have large and expensive military commitments abroad, but it has also undertaken to aid many countries in their progress toward higher standards of living. Moreover, many private citizens and corporations, pursuing diverse interests, have chosen to invest abroad. United States exports must be competitive enough not only to cover its imports, but also to provide the wherewithal for these other foreign expenditures.

There is no question that the competitive position of the United States in world markets continues to be strong. The relevant questions are, first, whether it is "strong enough" in the light of America's extensive commitments abroad and, second, whether this competitive strength has declined in recent years. The answer to the first question depends on the size of our present and future commitments abroad and on how large a deficit in its overall balance of payments the United States can or should run to provide the necessary liquidity for growth in world trade, without at the same time jeopardizing the international exchange standard.

With regard to the second question, there are unmistakable signs that the competitive trade position of the United States has indeed slipped somewhat in recent years. The relative decline in competitiveness in 1958 and 1959 was partly cyclical, but the tremendous recovery in exports in 1960 should not be allowed to conceal a definite weakening of the American position in world markets. The greater relative importance and the greater flexibility of raw-material prices abroad combine to cause a temporary decline in foreign manufacturing costs relative to American costs in periods of slack demand. Moreover, American businessmen are apparently less willing than their foreign counterparts to lower export prices in the face of excess productive capacity. This rigid pricing policy may account for the smaller decline in United States prices during the 1958 recession despite the greater decline in business activity in this country. In other words, foreign businessmen are more sensitive to the possibilities of maintaining production by marketing in other countries.

A purely cyclical decline in competitiveness is little cause for alarm. Concern *is* warranted over a possible secular deterioration in the competitive position — whether due to a declining lead in product improvement or to a tendency for prices of American exportable goods to rise faster than foreign export prices. Rising American costs seem to be due less to excessive wage increases relative to those abroad than to our very unimpressive improvement in labor productivity in manufacturing compared with that in many of the world's industrial countries. This in turn was due partly to the widespread introduction of up-to-date mass-production techniques in Europe — thus eliminating in some instances the advantage American producers had both in method and in scale of output — and partly to the willingness of European and Japanese business to invest on a vast scale quite apart from rationalization of existing plant. Prospects for a continuing rapid growth and the emergence of mass markets are perhaps the principal stimulus, demonstrating the well-known circularity in the process of growth and investment. Growing incomes and the coalescence of many countries into regional trading blocs such as the European Economic Community will perhaps lead to great increases in the volume of foreign industrial output. In many lines this rise in volume will lower unit costs still further.

The outlook for the United States is mixed. Continued rapid growth abroad is the best guarantee for high United States exports, a fact which reflects less on the competitive level of American production costs than on the constant pressure on production capacity abroad. But the American ability to export is still far from completely dependent on peak production shortages abroad; in an impressively wide range of goods American products are still preferred to those of foreign competitors. And the publicity which is now being focused on the importance of exports may increase the proclivity to think in "world" terms rather than merely in terms of the domestic market — to broaden horizons on the selling as well as the purchasing side. But the investment boom now taking place in Europe and Japan carries with it the possibility of further aggressive activity by these countries in world markets, perhaps at prices American firms will find difficult to meet.

What can the United States do? This is a subject for another essay and only a few remarks can be made here. It is certainly going too far to suggest at the present time, as one authority has done, that the United States needs to devalue its currency relative to the other principal currencies of the world in order to bring its prices back into line,[9] even if such a unilateral devaluation could be achieved. But it is taking too sanguine a view, in a world of managed currencies,

[9] See the remark by Theodore Yntema in the Report of the Committee for Economic Development, *National Objectives and the Balance of Payments Problems, 1960*, pp. 3–4.

to assume that everything will work itself out in the end. It is true that certain factors will work in that direction. Apart from the 5 per cent appreciation of the mark of early March, Germany is beginning to face a serious labor shortage for the first time since the war; skilled labor is also scarce in France and Japan. The pressure on wages abroad will mount. But productivity continues to rise, and if the pace of activity abroad slackens in the future, it may reveal a still further deterioration in the United States competitive position.

Rigorous anti-inflation policies, such as have been applied off and on during the past five years, may choke off the very investment which, while inflationary in the short run, is required to reduce costs of production and bring new products onto the market. As the British have learned during the entire postwar period, policies designed to reduce investment are always double-edged: while cutting current aggregate demand they also slow the flow of goods in the future. Both a broadened orientation toward foreign markets and increases in cost-reducing investment will be required if the United States is to maintain an export surplus large enough to cover its already huge financial commitments abroad.

RICHARD N. COOPER

The United States Competitive
Position—A 1965 Appraisal[*]

WHEN WE SPEAK about the competitive position of a country, or the competitiveness of its products in world markets, we are attempting to assess how well that country is doing in international trade, relative both to its own past and to the performance of other countries. I intend first to say something about the competitive performance of the United States, then to discuss several dimensions

    [*] From U.S. Senate, 89th Cong. Committee on Banking and Currency, *Hearings — Balance of Payments, 1965*, Part 1, pp. 418–27. Hereafter cited as *Balance of Payments, 1965*.

of competitiveness which I think are especially important, and finally to ask whether we can rely on further improvements in our competitive position to solve the balance of payments problem which currently confronts this country.

There is no question about the basic strength of America's overall competitive position. Total exports of goods and services from the United States reached $36.5 billion in 1964, far higher than had ever been recorded before [by] this or any other country. The United States provided over one-sixth of total world exports of merchandise. This country is, of course, also a heavy importer, and American imports of goods and services have grown by over $5 billion since 1960, paralleling the remarkable expansion of our gross national product. Despite this rapid rise in imports, however, the surplus of exports of goods and services over imports of goods and services has risen in every year since 1959, except for a slight fall in 1962; and in 1964 this surplus stood at $8.2 billion, the highest in our history except for the Second World War years of 1943 and 1944, and the postwar year of 1947 when the United States was exporting heavily to Europe and importing very little from that war-torn area. Of this surplus, $6.6 billion was provided by merchandise alone, and the remainder reflected for the most part our large earnings on foreign investment.

These figures include all exports of goods and services, including those financed by the American Government as part of our foreign aid program and those exports resulting from special government-to-government arrangements concerning the purchase of military equipment. If we make adjustments for these sales, the surplus is smaller, but the sharp and steady improvement over the past few years remains. On the definitions of the U. S. Treasury Department, our commercial surplus — that is, surplus adjusted for these Government-financed exports — grew from $3.7 billion in 1960 to $5.9 billion in 1964.

A substantial part of the growth in American exports and even in the growth of the trade surplus can be explained, of course, simply by the growth in world trade. World trade has grown exceptionally rapidly in recent years, rising in 1964 to $151 billion, 12 per cent above a year earlier and more than twice what it was 10 years ago. American exports have naturally participated in this rapid growth. At the same time, the U. S. economy, being relatively mature, has been growing more slowly than in many countries abroad, and U. S. imports have thus failed to grow as rapidly as world imports.

Recently, however, American exports have not merely kept up

with the growth in world trade. They have grown even more rapidly than total world exports, and as a consequence the U. S. share of world exports has increased slightly, after declining for many years. Analysis of export shares has become so fashionable these days that one tends to forget its limitations: (1) the strong influence of the particular dates chosen for comparison, (2) the paradoxical possibility that a country's export share can rise in every one of its markets and still decline in total, because of disparate rates of growth in these markets, and (3) the implicit but inappropriate normative implication that maintaining one's share in world markets is crucial or even important.

There are several reasons for believing that the U. S. share of world exports both would and should decline somewhat over time. The formation of large discriminatory free trade areas, such as the European Common Market, the European Free Trade Association, and the Latin American Free Trade Association, would naturally lead to a decline in America's share of world exports — though not necessarily in the total value of exports — as intraregional trade expands in response to lower internal trade barriers within these free trade areas.

Moreover, as incomes in the less developed countries of today rise, and as their economies become able to provide a wider range of goods of reasonable cost and quality, trade among them can be expected to increase. This trade is now extraordinarily low, accounting for well under 10 percent of world trade. An increase in trade among the less developed countries would be a salutary development, but it would lower U. S. export shares.

In spite of these reasons for some decline in American export shares, however, the share of American exports increased in 8 or 10 areas around the globe between the first half of 1963 and the first half of 1964, the latest period for which complete trade figures are available.

Moreover, the slight decline in the U. S. share of imports into Japan — which is one of the two areas in which our share did not rise — was due not to inroads from competitors in the European Common Market, but to a rising Japanese demand for materials from the less developed countries. Indeed, export shares of the European Common Market declined in a number of important regions during the same period.

These figures on the export surplus and export shares, taken all together, do not mark a country with a weak or a deteriorating competitive position. On the contrary, to many foreigners the competitive position of the United States is disconcertingly strong and is improving at an alarming rate, a theme to which I will return below.

We do not, of course, outcompete foreigners in all goods. Mutually beneficial international trade would not be possible on that basis. Some of our industries are bound to feel pressed by foreign competition. But overall, our performance has been very good.

If we look behind these indicators of competitive performance to the various factors which determine or influence the competitiveness of a country's products, we find evidence which is somewhat more difficult to evaluate. Competitive performance is determined by a number of factors — price, quality, design, delivery time, credit terms, servicing arrangements, and, not least, vigor of salesmanship. It is often difficult to determine which factors govern any particular sale.

There is, however, one dimension of competitiveness in which American performance has been unambiguously excellent. That is prices and, underlying prices, costs. U. S. wholesale prices of industrial goods are only half a per cent higher today than they were in 1959. Prices of intermediate industrial materials, important in American exports, have actually fallen since 1959, and prices of producer finished goods have risen by only 2½ percent. These price movements compare very favorably with price trends abroad. Since 1959 wholesale prices of industrial products have risen 15 percent in France, 12 percent in Italy, 9 percent in the Netherlands, 16 percent in Sweden, and 12 percent in the United Kingdom. Only Canada, Germany, and Japan maintained price records comparable to that of the United States, and German prices have begun to rise significantly during the past year.

These trends are quite different from those which prevailed in the preceding 5 years, 1954 to 1959. During that period U. S. prices rose substantially more than those of its major competitors, and the American export position weakened accordingly.

Comparisons of movements in domestic wholesale prices do not represent an ideal measure of price competitiveness, for two somewhat conflicting reasons.

First, the coverage of domestic wholesale prices does not represent accurately the composition of a country's exports — it is too broad in some respects, too narrow in others, and it often includes the prices of imported goods. For the purposes of assessing changes in our price competitiveness, we badly need an accurate index of export prices, as was recommended some years ago in the Stigler report to the Budget Bureau on "The Price Statistics of the Federal Goverment." We still do not have such an index.

We can get a very rough indication of export price performance, however, from figures compiled by the United Nations on the "unit value of exports of manufacture" from the major exporting nations. These show less divergence from country to country than do the movements in wholesale prices of industrial products, as might be expected given the stiff competition in international markets. Nonetheless, export "unit values" have risen more rapidly in most major countries during the past few years than they have for the United States. The major exceptions, again, are Canada, whose devaluations in 1961 and 1962 lowered export unit values about 8 percent, and Japan, which has experienced steadily falling export prices for many years.

The second defect in wholesale price indexes as a measure of price competitiveness is the one to which I just alluded: In a highly competitive world wholesale prices cannot diverge very much from country to country. It is necessary, therefore, to undertake the more difficult task of examining movements in costs rather than prices. Here again the U. S. performance has been good. Hourly earnings of workers in industry rose only 19 percent in the United States between 1958 and 1964, compared with increases of 29 percent in Belgium and Britain, 56 percent in France, 58 percent in Germany, 61 percent in the Netherlands, 70 percent in Italy, and 70 percent in Japan.

These vast differences in wage increases reflect largely, of course, differences in the growth in productivity from country to country. But when allowance is made for that, labor costs rose substantially less in the United States than they did in most other countries. A recent study by the Bureau of Labor Statistics shows that between 1959 and 1962 labor costs per unit of output in manufacturing rose by only 2 percent in the United States, compared with 13 percent in Britain, 23 percent in Germany, 9 percent in Japan, and (for production workers only) 9 percent in France, 6 percent in Italy, and 16 percent in Sweden. Wage increases have been outstripping increases in productivity handsomely in most countries since 1962, so this trend toward higher costs abroad has continued.

It is sometimes suggested that comparisons of percentage increases for wages are not appropriate, since foreign wage levels are so much lower than they are in the United States. Thus a 10-percent increase in $1 an hour is absolutely less than a 5-percent increase in $2.54 per hour, which was the average hourly earning in U. S. manufacturing industries in 1964.

This observation is arithmetically correct, but it is analytically irrelevant. Broadly speaking, the level of wages in each country reflects its productivity; if wages are higher in the United States than elsewhere, that is because productivity is also higher. I once estimated average productivity per man-hour in manufacturing for a number of countries for the year 1959 and found it to vary from $3.89 in the United States to about $0.40 in Japan, with the European countries clustered around $1 per hour. . . . Japanese firms cannot, of course, afford to pay their workers even $0.75 per hour if their average net output is only $0.40 per hour.

Productivity abroad has gone up rapidly since 1959, so these figures are now somewhat out of date. But the basic point remains that movements in unit labor costs are the result of relative changes in wages and productivity, not of absolute changes in wages alone. If the general level of wages rises by the same percentage in two countries and productivity remains unchanged, the rise in unit labor costs will be about the same regardless of disparities in the wage levels unless unit labor costs differ substantially between the two countries at the outset.

As the preceding observations indicate, American performance in the areas of price and cost competitiveness has been very good during the past few years, the compound effect of stability at home and rising prices and costs abroad. Recently some analysts have become alarmed by the very sharp rise in certain raw materials prices which has taken place during the past 15 months, and have suggested that this rise in prices may threaten the ability of American exports to compete in world markets. I would like to suggest, to the contrary, that a general rise in materials prices, by itself, will help rather than hurt the U. S. balance of payments. There are four reasons for this.

The first and most obvious, but possibly the least important, is that the United States is itself a substantial exporter of industrial materials and therefore benefits directly, in the short run, from higher prices for such products as aluminum, sulphur, phosphates, oilseeds, and so on. Europe and Japan, by contrast, export only very small amounts of industrial materials and import them heavily.

Second, higher materials prices mean higher foreign exchange receipts to primary producing countries, including Canada as well as many less developed countries. In the past these countries have spent a higher-than-average share of increases in earnings on purchases from the United States. This should be considered in conjunction with the fact that Europe and Japan together are much larger importers of industrial materials than is the United States, so much of the additional earnings of the primary producing countries will come from Europe and Japan, while much of the additional expenditures by these countries will be made in the United States. And, of course, earnings on U. S. investments in primary producing countries will rise.

Third, some evidence suggests that a given rise in prices of industrial materials will raise the manufacturing costs of our major competitors more than it will raise U. S. manufacturing costs, because materials account for a larger share of total unit costs abroad than in the United States. A survey of comparable firms in the United States and abroad by the National Industrial Conference Board showed materials accounting for an average of 46 percent of total manufacturing costs in the European Common Market, for instance, compared with 32 percent in this country. . . . Similar relationships prevailed for other countries.

For the same reason, Europe benefited substantially from the weakness in primary product prices following 1960, for this helped offset the gradual rise in labor costs taking place there. Merely halting the fall in materials prices therefore increased the cost pressures on European firms. Rising materials prices will increase those cost pressures on foreign firms relative to the cost pressures on American firms.

Finally, when materials prices do rise they tend to rise more rapidly in international markets, where European purchases are made, than in the tariff-sheltered and largely domestically supplied market in the United States. This factor, to which I would attach some but not a great deal of significance, will put still further pressures on European and Japanese costs in a period of rising prices and conversely in a period of falling prices.

Putting all these factors together, higher materials prices should strengthen the U. S. trade position, even after allowing for the higher prices which American firms would admittedly have to pay for their own imports of raw materials.

I have dealt at some length on price and cost factors in our competitive position. A number of economists are inclined to give these second place in importance compared with the quality of American goods and in particular with the invention and production of new and advanced products. According to this view, the United States draws its export strength in manufactures not so much from lower prices and costs as from a continual outpouring of new and advanced products which are not available elsewhere — from a technological lead which gives the United States a momentary advantage until other countries begin to produce identical or competing goods. And by that time Americans have devised still newer and better products.

In terms of this argument, the weakening competitive position of the United States during the 1950's can be explained by an erosion of this technological lead. Other countries began to develop new products themselves, and they began to produce new American products more quickly following their initial development here. You may remember the quip several years ago expressing this change. In January, an American invents a wonderful new product, in February the Russians claim they invented it in 1935, and by March the Japanese are exporting it to the United States.

It is not difficult to appreciate the reasons for any diminution of America's technological lead which may have taken place. Other countries have become highly alert to the benefits of research and development expenditures and to advanced technical education, and they have stepped up their programs in both areas. France quite explicitly bases a part of its case for maintaining an atomic weapons program — and for its joint efforts with Britain to produce the supersonic airliner Concorde — on the "technological fallout" which large programs such as this can generate. Countries which want to remain in the technological forefront feel they must have active and popular programs which attract high quality personnel to the technological frontier and keep them there. I do not pass judgment on these arguments, but only note that they are given important consideration abroad. The concern of Britain and others about the "brain drain" arises in part from the same considerations.

A second factor tending to reduce the technological lead of the United States is the very rapid growth in American direct investment abroad, especially in Europe. Direct investment outflows from the United States to Europe have grown from $190 million in 1958 to over $1,200 million in 1964, a sixfold increase in 6 years. With American capital go American management skills and American know-how. Indeed, increasingly these factors have been exported even in the absence of direct investment in productive facilities abroad. In 1964 the United States earned about $1 billion in royalties and fees for rights to produce patented American products, for technical and managerial advice from American firms, and the like. Only two-thirds of these receipts came from U. S. subsidiaries abroad. We are engaging increasingly in the export of knowledge per se, disembodied from American goods and from American capital.

I regard this as one of the most far reaching of recent developments in international trade. While the United States benefits directly from the sale of this knowledge, such sales do cut the technological lead of American industry further and increase foreign competition with many American products. It is worth recalling that exporting knowledge was not always so easy. In medieval Europe severe restrictions were often placed on the movements of skilled craftsmen, lest they take their trade secrets to rival cities. And it was not until 1843 that Britain removed its prohibition on the export of textile machinery — a prohibition designed to preserve Britain's primacy as a manufacturing center by withholding up-to-date capital equipment from would be foreign competitors. A legacy of these limitations on the movement of technical knowledge is found today in our own restrictions on exports to the Soviet bloc, restrictions which extend well beyond products of direct military value.

The recent improvement in the American competitive position has taken place despite increasing attention abroad to the application of new technology. I do not know how to assess the net value to the United States in the long run of exporting our technology. Certainly from a global viewpoint it is desirable. But it will reduce our export sales of some products.

There are many other dimensions of competitiveness. I will say something briefly about only one more, credit terms, because it is a dimension of competitiveness which is of particular interest to this committee. The level of interest rates and credit availability which we maintain in this country influence among other things the cost of export credit. A rise in interest rates at home will stiffen the credit terms which American exporters offer their customers. British exporters have castigated Britain's frequent reliance on increases in interest rates for this reason. A report by the Federation of British Industries points out that —

it is a disagreeable paradox that steps to protect the currency at a time of crisis in the balance of payments can in themselves increase the difficulties of expanding exports —

and this report urges the British Government to pursue a policy of lower and more stable interest rates (Export Incentives, 1962).

So far, being able to offer favorable credit terms has aided American exporters. The rise in American interest rates over the last year and a half may not have impeded exports much because foreign interest rates have also risen. To that extent of course, the United States did not improve its balance-of-payments position by raising interest rates either.

Some countries attempt to mitigate the deleterious effect of higher interest rates and tighter credit on exports by providing special facilities for export credit, such as the rediscounting privileges for export paper at the central banks in France and Italy and the French exemption for export credit from the 10 percent credit ceilings which have been imposed since September 1963. While these measures are easy to understand — the United States has taken steps to insure that the interest equalization tax will not limit our exports — we should avoid pursuing the dangerous and self-defeating path in which one country after another tightens credit at home and then introduces special rates for export credit which represent in effect, export subsidies, since they make it easier for domestic firms to sell abroad than at home. Such a policy would be costly to growth without benefit to the balance of payments.

As I have already indicated, the U. S. trade position is very strong, it has been improving, and at least some of the factors which determine a country's competitive position continue to work in favor of further improvement. That is good, and it is important for our balance of payments. We should avoid measures which weaken our competitive position. At the same time, I think that the emphasis currently placed on increasing exports still further as a principal means to correct the payments deficit is inappropriate. We must remember two things: the basic symmetry in international trade and the large size and relative importance of the United States in world trade. The first means that any improvement in the competitive position of the United States — any further increase in the already huge American surplus — necessarily involves a deterioration in the current account balance of other countries. The second point means that any significant improvement in the U. S. position will be substantial in size and noticeable in the accounts of others, not negligible as it might be for improvements in the trade balance of, say, the Philippines or even of India. These countries can plan on expanding export markets without the need for others to take it much into account. The same is not true for the United States.

The underlying symmetry in international accounts and the preponderant size of the United States must be set against the attitudes which other nations have taken toward their own trade positions during the past few years. Canada, the most important trading partner of the United States, has an announced objective of reducing its dependence for external balance on capital inflows by eliminating its current account deficit — which arises largely from its transactions with the United States — over the next few years. It has already moved very far in this direction, reducing its current account deficit from $1.5 billion in 1959 to under $0.5 billion in 1964. Some Canadians point to the time when Canada would become a net exporter of capital, with a corresponding current account surplus — rather than a deficit as it has had — as would seem consistent with its wealth and per capita income.

British officials have for years spoken of the need to raise Britain's current account surplus to 300 pounds sterling ($840 million) annually — a very large increase from the present level — to cover its large oversea financial committments and to build up its dangerously low reserves. Japan's trade position has improved very greatly during the past year, but Japanese officials continue to be concerned with strengthening Japan's competitive position too, partly to meet new international competition as it undertakes further trade liberalization, partly to reduce its current account deficit of roughly $0.5 billion a year and to reduce its large external indebtedness.

Even the European Economic Community, whose members collectively have been accumulating reserves at an incredible rate and who have been claiming gold from the United States, has expressed alarm at the sharp deterioration in its own trade position during the past few years. The trade balance of the EEC with the rest of the world slipped from virtual balance in 1960 to a deficit of $3 billion in 1963 and of $2.3 billion in the first 9 months of 1964, despite the sharp downturn in Italy which took place last year. Credit restraint, already severe in Italy and France, is being applied increasingly in other members of the EEC largely in response to this deterioration and to the related increase in prices.

We find the same story with other countries. Switzerland is very much worried about the vulnerability inherent in a huge current account deficit balanced — sometimes overbalanced — by a massive inflow of short-term funds. The less developed countries, too, all want to improve their export earnings; but fortunately we can depend on them to spend these earnings for debt repayment or badly needed imports rather than accumulate them as reserves for more than short periods of time.

It is clear that not all countries can succeed in realizing these inconsistent objectives at the same time. Some of them are bound to be frustrated. The United States, with its already huge surplus, is in an especially weak position to argue that it needs the improvement most. As I indicated earlier, the American surplus might in fact rise somewhat further as a result of favorable movements in costs and prices which have already taken place and will continue in the near future. But additional measures to increase it further will meet both resentment and resistance from our major trading partners. Such measures are likely to be thwarted by countermeasures taken by others to stimulate their exports, by stiff opposition to further reductions in trade barriers, and possibly even by increased barriers to trade. I do not think that we can rely on that route to solve our balance-of-payments problem. We must look instead to the capital account for substantial improvement.

JOHN J. ARENA

Is the United States Pricing Itself Out of World Markets?*

THE DEFICIT in the U. S. balance of international payments is a problem of widespread concern today. One commonly proposed method for eliminating the deficit is to sell more abroad, but such a solution depends on our ability to meet and beat foreign competition in world markets. The real question then is: How competitive are we?

This paper presents some evidence to help answer this question insofar as it pertains to consumer products. A study was made of about 200 consumer goods, excluding automobiles, representing over 2,400 different product brands from 1950 through 1964. Two indexes (one for U. S. markets and one for the foreign markets) were computed showing the competitive position of U. S.- and foreign-made goods. These were examined to see whether our ability to compete improved or declined over this time period. They showed that in U. S. markets the competitiveness of American consumer goods deteriorated during the 1950's but stabilized after 1960. In foreign markets, however, our position has sharply deteriorated since 1960.

In 1964 the United States sold abroad about $26 billion of goods,

* From John J. Arena, "Is the United States Pricing Itself Out of World Markets?" *New England Business Review*, July 1965, pp. 2–6. Reprinted by permission of the Federal Reserve Bank of Boston.

ranging from agricultural commodities to heavy manufacturing equipment. Of this total approximately 13 per cent could be classified as consumer goods such as bicycles, cameras, washing machines, radios, and a host of others. The demand for such goods appears to be growing. The Western European countries, particularly those in the Common Market, seem to be on the verge of a consumer goods boom similar to that in the United States in the immediate postwar period and the 1950's. Rapidly rising incomes and a taste for the "good life" are enabling the broad mass of Western Europeans to enjoy the fruits of a consumer economy. Opportunities for sales of such goods to Europe, therefore, look promising. The question, however, is: How effectively can we compete there?

Price is, of course, the most obvious form of competitiveness, and the lowest priced product should have an important advantage. As Chart I shows, prices in the United States have been moving up slowly while those abroad have advanced more rapidly. Thus, one may be tempted to conclude that our ability to sell in foreign markets has improved. But, in fact, there is the question of whether or not these published price indexes are applicable to internationally traded goods or only to goods in general. It is quite possible that while prices abroad have been rising, as in Chart I, the prices of goods that actually enter international trade have been stable, if not declining.

Price indexes in any one country measure the prices of consumer goods that are important in that country. For example, in the United States automobile prices are more important and food prices less important components of the consumer price index than in less developed countries. Thus, aggregate price indexes in different countries are not comparable because of differences in the products they measure and the weights given to each product. Thus, as the sole criterion of international competitiveness, reliance on broadly-based consumer price information can be misleading.

Prices, however, are clearly not the only forms of competition in international trade. Many factors such as style, workmanship, availability of service, etc., enter the buying decision and must be included in studies of competitiveness.

In this study, therefore, both price and quality factors were included for a sample of goods that directly enter international trade. The measure of quality used here was based on tests made by such rating services as *Consumer Bulletin, Consumer Report,* both of which are published monthly in the United States, and *Which?*, a monthly publication of the United Kingdom. These services con-

CHART I — COST OF LIVING INDEXES

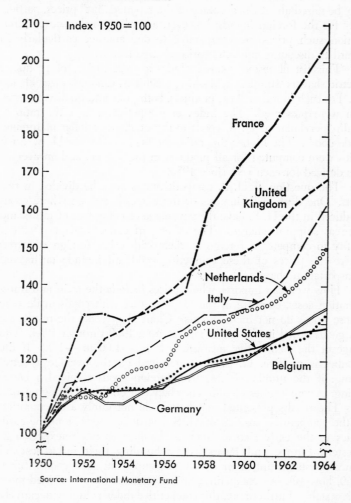

Index 1950=100

France

United Kingdom

Netherlands

Italy

United States

Belgium

Germany

Source: International Monetary Fund

sider not only price but a host of other factors. Since 1950 about 200 tests have been made in which U. S. brands were compared directly with foreign-made brands.

These goods are products which are actually sold in world markets and whose dollar sales prices are reported. Some question may be raised about the accuracy of the reported "list" prices, particularly for the foreign brands; however, according to the source information such prices are comparable to one another particularly in regard to discounts and other price change factors.

This list of tested goods includes a great variety of products: electric shavers, sunglasses, washing machines, cameras, razor blades, etc. For each brand of these products, both price and quality information were presented. The index of competitiveness is the ratio of quality-per-dollar of U. S. goods to the quality-per-dollar of foreign-made goods. The higher this ratio, the better off is the U. S. Such ratios were computed for all products in the sample, and an average was derived for each year since 1950.

The question of U. S. competitiveness must be divided in two parts. One deals with imports or the domestic market where goods produced in the U. S. have the advantage of being free of tariffs and overseas shipping charges. The other part concerns exports or our ability to compete in foreign markets with other foreign countries where the prices of these competing goods all include tariffs and transportation charges.

How well can imports, whose prices *include* the tariff and transportation costs, compete in the U. S. market with goods made here whose prices do not include costs? Chart II presents the results for the goods tested in the U. S. market from 1950 through 1964. The range of the competitive measure is from —1.00 to +1.00. If the number is positive, U. S. goods received on the average a better rating; if the number is negative, foreign goods received a better rating. A zero implies no difference between U. S. and foreign goods.

The results presented in Chart II do not imply a deterioration in the competitive position of U. S. consumer goods from the early fifties to the early sixties. Such a change was not unexpected as Western Europe and Japan were rebuilding their industries and hence re-establishing their ability to compete in such goods. Since 1960, however, our competitive ability seems to have remained more or less stable. Furthermore, this competitive index is highly negatively correlated with the value of United States' imports of the goods in question. The higher the index for a given product (i.e., the better this country's competitive position) the more we seem to export and the less to import.

Chart II also presents a series on our competitive ability abroad. Because of lack of data this series is for a shorter time period. It depicts the ability of the U. S. to sell consumer goods in the United Kingdom, as compared to that of all other foreign countries that sell in the U. K. *except* the U. K. In this way, a measure is provided of the ability of the U. S. to compete in so-called third-country markets where *both* the U. S. and foreign goods must bear the import and

CHART II — COMPETITIVE MEASURES OF U.S. GOODS*

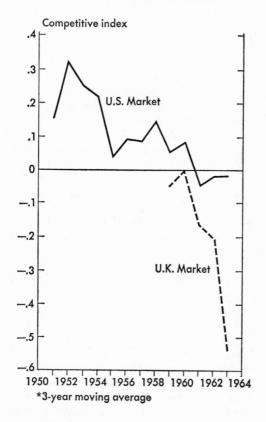

*3-year moving average

transportation charges. (Goods produced in the U. K. were, therefore, excluded in this test since they do not bear these extra charges.) The results of this series imply a much greater deterioration in the

U. S. competitive position than that shown for the U. S. market. Part of this decline is attributable to the growing favorable tariff treatment received by the European Free Trade Association countries (as compared to the U. S.) whose products were well represented in the tests.

Certain products were examined more than once over the test period. For the U. S. market, 17 such products showed a deterioration, while 15 showed an improvement. However, the products which declined had on the average a bigger absolute change than those which improved. Thus, Chart II and the results of the retests are compatible; both imply a deterioration in competitive ability. The few U. K. market retests all showed a deterioration in the U. S. competitive position which closely parallels the results in Chart II.

What has caused the deterioration or improvement, as the case may be, in our competitive position for these retested products? No complete answer is readily available but the evidence implies that, in cases where our position has improved, the dominant factor has been the superiority of our product quality (probably from our high rate of innovation) rather than a lower price. Conversely, where our position has declined, not only has foreign quality improved but foreign prices have declined relative to ours. This could be the result of catching up in terms of goods produced as well as cost reductions derived from economies of scale.

In view of this information, the outlook for the growth of exports of consumer goods may appear gloomy. It should be emphasized, however, that people do not buy simply according to the ratings of testing agencies, that consumer goods are only a small fraction of our total exports, and that the demand for such goods is growing. Also we produce many other goods quite inexpensively. Agricultural products, particularly wheat, are an area in which we have a very favorable competitive advantage (ignoring tariff and quota problems).

In addition, our innovations frequently lead to the development of unique products or products with unique features, e.g., a camera which uses cartridge-type film. Such goods often have a high demand and initially at least can only be produced in the United States. Further efforts to achieve uniqueness of product as well as improvement in quality can help offset the decline in the consumer goods part of our foreign trade.

However, it should be noted that this innovating effort seems to be more fruitful in goods other than the consumer goods examined here. Specialized machinery, new chemical products, aircraft equipment, etc., are all examples of such products. While we have declined in competitiveness for consumer products, we have improved in these other areas as can be seen by our healthy trade surplus. Better and new products are the key to U. S. competitiveness. The results of the retested items bear this out.

The evidence of this analysis shows that our competitive ability in consumer goods has suffered a relative decline in the domestic market since the early fifties but has become stable since 1960. However, since 1960 an even sharper deterioration has occurred in foreign markets.

Because of increasing affluence abroad, however, particularly in the European countries, the outlook for the demand of consumer goods products seems good. Thus, our sales of consumer goods abroad could remain high or even increase, but they would be still larger if our competitive position could stay stable or improve.

H. PETER GRAY

International Trade in Invisible Items

MOST DISCUSSIONS and analyses of international trade flows either confine themselves to, or deal primarily with, international trade in commodities. It is easy to see why this should be so: there is a more direct realization that an imported car reduces domestic automobile products (and jobs) and that an exported machine has increased domestic gross national product than that a vacation in Japan has taken money out of the country. Secondly, tariffs have been a perennial bone of international contention and, while you can levy a tariff on a commodity import, it is difficult to tax international trade in services. Finally, commodity trade has been more important in terms of value than invisible trade and, until recently, commodity trade constituted nearly all international trade. However, if an economy can gain from trade in commodities there is no logical reason why world welfare cannot also be increased by the international exchange of services and, as in the domestic economy, services are becoming increasingly important in international trade.

The simplest measure of the relative importance of invisible trade to commodity trade is to compare the value of imports and exports of the two categories. In 1951 service trade of the United States amounted to $7.2 billion or 28.5 percent of the value of trade in commodities: in 1964 the value of exports and imports of services was $18 billion and amounted to 40 percent of commodity trade.[1]

There are three main items which make up the bulk of invisible trade: interest and dividend flows, foreign travel, and transportation. There is also a catch-all category understandably called "miscellaneous services."

Interest and dividend credits are payments made to residents of the United States (and therefore equivalent to exports) as a result of their ownership of foreign assets. For example, if the Ford Motor Company of England makes a profit and sends this profit back to its parent company, the United States receives a dividend credit. Profits retained abroad by a subsidiary firm are not included in the balance of payments even though they represent an increase in the net foreign wealth of United States residents. Similarly an outflow of dollars takes place when a nonresident receives a dividend check from an American corporation or an interest payment on a United States Treasury bond.

Clearly the volume of these flows depends very largely upon the volume of investment made in foreign countries in the historic past. The United States has been a net international creditor since World War I — i.e., foreign assets owned by United States residents including the federal government have exceeded claims on American corporations, etc., held by foreigners. Since that time the United States has steadily increased its net ownership of foreign assets despite occasional expropriations. Interest and dividend credits (exports) consequently exceed debits by a significant amount. In 1964 the United States received $3.74 billion from past direct investment[2] and $1.7 billion from other investments. Total payments by the United States amounted to $1.4 billion in the same year. Because of the high rate of foreign investment undertaken by the United States in

[1] Military expenditures abroad are not included in these computations. The data were taken from *Survey of Current Business*.

[2] Direct investment may be defined as investment in real assets as opposed to other investments in paper claims, e.g., foreign bonds.

the last twenty years the net credit on this account may be expected to increase with time. However, to the extent that this foreign investment is not financed by a surplus on current account but by foreign short-term investment in the United States, the potential increase in the surplus on this account will be diminished by larger payments to foreigners.

The direct investments of the United States are not evenly distributed throughout the world. Over half of these assets by value are located in the western hemisphere and approximately one quarter in Western Europe. However, the rate of investment in Western Europe is increasing and accounted for approximately half of the total foreign direct investment in 1962 — this surge being greatly influenced by Europe's rapid rate of growth and the formation of the Common Market which induced American manufacturers to open manufacturing facilities behind the tariff wall.

Foreign investment involves an outflow of dollars and promises to yield a stream of balance-of-payments credits in the future. But the capital outflow may not be the only balance-of-payments cost involved. The foreign productive capacity created by the investment can serve as a domestic source of supply to displace American exports and can also compete with American-made goods in third countries or even in the United States.[3]

American know-how can be exported without an accompanying capital flow if the know-how is sold to a foreign entrepreneur under a licensing agreement. Arrangements of this kind are similar to direct foreign investment in that they can lead to the replacement of American exports by domestic production as well as to a stream of balance-of-payments credits in the future. The stream of payments will, of course, be smaller relative to sales, since they will not include a return on the physical capital. In 1963, United States receipts from management fees and royalties amounted to more than $500 million.[4]

Foreign travel by American residents accounts for more than 11 per cent of total payments on current account in 1964. The desire to visit faraway places with strange-sounding names needs no explanation although it should be remembered that foreign travel account includes expenditures made by businessmen and students as well as

[3] For a discussion of the impact of United States foreign investment on the balance of payments see Walter S. Salant, et al, *The United States Balance of Payments in 1968* (Washington, D.C.: The Brookings Institution, 1963), pp. 142–147.

[4] For detailed information on United States foreign investments and the related flows see *Survey of Current Business* (August 1963), pp. 16–22.

those of tourists. Visitors to the United States counteract this outflow to some extent but American earnings from foreign visitors are relatively small if Canadian expenditures are excluded. In 1964 all foreign travel resulted in a net outflow of approximately $1½ billion out of gross imports in the amount of $2.85 billion.

Foreign travel gives rise to two distinct types of expenditure: money actually spent abroad and the cost of getting there. All monies spent abroad are imports of services from foreigners and it is this sum which is reported under "foreign travel" account in the United States balance of payments. Transportation costs only enter into the balance of payments if the fare is paid to a foreign-flag carrier: e.g., if an American decides to spend a week in Paris and spends $400 for his fare and $200 in Paris, the whole $600 will be an import (a debit in the balance of payments) if he flies by Air France, but only $200 will be imported if he flies by Pan American or by TWA.

As might be expected, foreign travel is a luxury.[5] Estimates of the demand of Americans for foreign travel (including fare payments to foreign flag carriers) show that an increase of one dollar in American disposable income will give rise to an increase in imports of one and a quarter cents.[6] A growth rate in the United States of about 5 percent per annum would increase disposable income in a single year by approximately $20 billion and tourist imports by $250 million. Thus, payments on travel account may be expected to increase rapidly and to constitute a significant import leakage in the future. Nor is the potential dollar outflow easily rectified except by such extreme action as the impositions of restrictions on the availability of foreign currency for travel purposes. A recent suggestion of the Johnson Administration was to impose an export tax of $100 on Americans who wished to leave the country. This suggestion evoked a wave of protests of such magnitude that the suggestion was dropped. Two other attempts have been made to reduce the net ouflow on travel account: the United States travel service was created to promote foreign tourism in the United States and the duty-free allowance on commodities purchased abroad by travelers has been reduced in two stages from $500 (wholesale value) to $100 (retail value). United States receipts have approximately doubled since 1954, amounting to $1.2 billion in 1964. Both measures will have helped to reduce the rate of growth of the deficit on travel account but neither can be expected to reverse the trend.

[5] In economics a good is a luxury if an increase in income results in a greater than proportional increase in expenditure on that good.

[6] See H. Peter Gray, "The Demand for International Travel by the United States and Canada," *International Economic Review* (1966), pp. 83–92.

While it can be misleading to look at individual items in the balance of payments because total demand for American exports depends upon the ability of other countries to pay for them, and therefore on American imports, foreign travel is a serious negative item because of the geographic distribution of our expenditures. If money is spent in a country which is importing as much as it can and which imports a large proportion of these imports from the United States, then the bigger the travel deficit with this country the greater the value of other exports. Thus, a deficit with Canada is not as damaging to the overall balance of payments as would be an equal deficit with France or West Germany. In fact, more than one half of the travel deficit in 1964 was incurred with Western European countries.

The United States began the post-World War II era with substantial advantages (and surplus) on transportation account. However the rebuilding of foreign merchant fleets decimated during the war and the higher operating costs of United States ships have eliminated the United States advantage on ocean shipping completely. Similarly, the share of the international market enjoyed by United States international airlines has declined as a result of the establishment of many new national airlines. Consequently, transportation account has changed from a surplus of $1,150 million in 1947 to a deficit of $150 million in 1964.

The relative loss of receipts from ocean shipping can be attributed almost entirely to the higher wage costs of American crews being unmatched by an equal productivity advantage so that as the increase in world tonnage reduced shipping rates, American ships were priced out of the market and mothballed. The subsidies paid to the United States merchant marine are limited in scope and designed from a national defense point of view so that their balance-of-payment impact is less than it might be.[7]

The deficit on passenger transportation can be traced to the large tourist deficit as well as to the decrease in the proportion of total flights scheduled by United States carriers. The greater the excess of travel imports by Americans over those of foreign residents, the greater must be the share of total receipts of United States carriers if a deficit is to be avoided. Yet, while the share of total expenditures on routes to and from the United States received by American lines has declined from 69 percent in 1951 to 52 percent in 1960, the

[7] For example, subsidies are limited to freighters with scheduled ports of call and any freighter learning of a profitable cargo which would require leaving that schedule must refuse it or lose his subsidy.

share of expenditures paid by United States travelers has increased from 64 to 69 percent.

Miscellaneous services account includes management fees, royalties, film rentals, earnings and expenditures of the United States government, payments to foreign workers in the United States (debit) and expenditures in the United States of foreign workers, employees of foreign governments and international institutions as well as the expenditures of the governments and institutions themselves (credit).[8]

This account has shown a considerable and growing surplus which amounted to $860 million in 1963 — largely due to the receipts of management fees and royalties.

In summary, invisible trade is quantitatively important to both the United States and the rest of the world. From the point of view of the United States balance of payments, the question is whether the two accounts with growing surpluses will increase sufficiently to offset the two deficit accounts: so far the return on foreign investment has been increasing fast enough to yield an ever-increasing surplus on total invisible trade.

LAWRENCE B. KRAUSE

European Economic Integration and the United States[*]

INTRODUCTION

For the second time in the twentieth century, a new area is dominating international trade. Just as the United States eclipsed Great Britain as the world's largest trading nation in the early part of the century, so is the European Economic Community outpacing

[8] While the United States government has a deficit on international account, the United States enjoyed a surplus on total government account as expenditures in the United States by foreign governments and institutions more than exceed the federal government's nonmilitary deficit.

[*] From Lawrence B. Krause, "European Economic Integration and the United States," American Economic Review, Vol. LXIII, No. 2 (May 1963), pp. 185–96. Reprinted by permission of the author and the American Economic Association.

the United States today. The exports and imports of the Common Market represent 24% of world trade (including intra-Community trade) while the U. S. percentage is only 16%. The members of the European Economic Community maintain their separate political identities, but for questions of international commerce, they must be treated as a single unit since they make unified decisions with respect to commercial policy. If all the countries currently applying for membership in the EEC were to be accepted, then the United States would be relatively small by comparison.

The formation of the European Economic Community has not only redefined trade statistics, it has and is changing the patterns of world trade. In 1958, the last year before tariff preferences were begun, less than 30% of the imports of the member countries originated in other member countries. In 1961, just three years later, 36% of the imports of the member countries came from other members. Looked at from the other side, exports of the EEC countries to nonmembers increased by only 29% between 1958 and 1961 while their exports to each other increased by 73%.

The economic success of the Common Market has been demonstrated not only by the remarkable increases in trade, but also by the fact that the dismantling of internal restrictions to trade has been appreciably accelerated. With the reaching of an agreement on the beginning of a common agricultural policy, the EEC has moved into the second transitional stage of the Rome Treaty. Because of the very success of the Common Market in its economic objectives, it has become even more necessary to evaluate the EEC as to its effects on nonmember countries.

THE EEC AS A POLITICAL MECHANISM

It has been a unanimous observation of all analysts of the EEC that the effects of European integration for nonmembers cannot be determined by studying the Rome Treaty alone. As much or more will depend on the administration of the provisions and subsequent policy decisions that put its ideas into practice. Since these subsequent policy decisions while economic in character are determined within the particular *political* institutions of the EEC, some evaluation of the political mechanism is required to make judgments as to eventual outcomes.

It must be recalled that the determining motivations for the formation of a Common Market among the original six countries were primarily political in character. The desire to institutionalize the Franco-German *rapprochement;* the need to give an outlet to West

German nationalism through the goal of wider European unity; and the attraction of combining the individual national powers into a large "third force" that could stand on the same level and, independent of the United States and the Soviet Union, were probably much more important in bringing about the Rome Treaty than the expected economic gains of membership in an exclusive trading group. The vehicle chosen for furthering these political objectives was an economic union because of the willingness of the prospective member countries to accept this type of divestiture of national sovereignty as evidenced by the Coal and Steel Community and corresponding reluctance to join a political union as indicated by the defeat of the European Defense Community.

Certain consequences follow directly from using economic means for political ends. When questions arise as to the treatment of nonmember countries, there is always a political motive for discriminating against nonmembers even if no great economic interest is at stake because the economic benefits of membership cannot be weakened without undermining the political unity that it is intended to cement. The common external tariff, for instance, is more than a means of protecting industry of the member countries from outside competition; it is the tie that binds the countries together. This suggests that the EEC may be unwilling to reduce their external tariffs to zero unless progress is made toward political unity through other means.

In sharp contrast to the substantial progress that the EEC has made on the economic front, the development of political unity has been minimal. The institutional framework provided for in the Rome Treaty is just sufficient to enable the customs union to operate but nothing more. The center of power rests in the Council of Ministers and the ministers are representatives of the member countries. Unanimous consent is required for practically all issues.[1] With such a system, implying as it does a veto power by all members, decision making is slow, very cumbersome, and extremely painful. An exact balance of national interests must be obtained before agreement can be reached on any issue. In the decision process, little if any weight is given to the interests of countries not represented at the bargaining table because of these difficulties. Problems of nonmember countries that resulted from the creation of the EEC, therefore, are unlikely to receive attention by the Council of Ministers because nothing gets

[1] The Rome Treaty provides that some issues are to be settled through qualified majority voting in the Council of Ministers, and the number of issues so determined are to increase with successive stages within the transitional period. So far no issue of any consequence has been determined by majority voting.

decided unless it poses a crisis for the Community itself or for one of the member countries. Furthermore, once agreement on an issue has been reached, it is next to impossible to get the Council of Ministers to reconsider their decision because they are unwilling to open old wounds. This is true despite some adverse consequences of the policy for nonmember countries.

ECONOMIC IMPLICATIONS OF THE EEC FOR THE UNITED STATES

The importance of the political bias against the economic interest of nonmember countries depends in part on what effects the Community is likely to have on excluded countries. For the United States, this question can be analyzed by looking at the consequences of the EEC on the bilateral trade between the U. S. and the EEC and also at its consequences on our trade with third countries. For this purpose, United States exports to the Common Market can be divided into three groups: industrial products, agricultural products, and non-agricultural raw materials.

U. S. EXPORTS OF INDUSTRIAL PRODUCTS

Unlike trade in agricultural products, the Common Market has made relatively few changes in the institutional system whereby industrial goods are imported into member countries. A tariff is levied on industrial products when imported from nonmembers, but this has always been the case. The new element arises from the fact that goods coming from other member countries will not have to pay a tariff or be restricted in any way and the tariff barrier to the outside world will be uniform regardless to which member country the import is sent.[2] The consequences of this system for nonmembers depend on how much protection the external tariff wall provides as compared to the previously existing national tariffs. The common external tariff was calculated by taking an unweighted average of the French, German, Italian, and Benelux tariffs (with some exceptions).[3] The

[2] During the transitional period, existing barriers on intra-Community trade will be gradually reduced and finally eliminated.

[3] This average led to tariffs somewhat on the high side because of the un-weighted feature and also because the national tariffs used in the calculation were above those actually in force on January 1, 1958. The German tariff which was averaged excluded the 25% tariff reduction of August 1957. The rate chosen for Italy excluded the tariff reductions of 1951. Also a Benelux tariff on most chemicals of 12% was averaged in, although no such tariff was in force. Rome Treaty, Article 19 (2). Article 19 (3) (d) and List E.

protectiveness of the tariff cannot be determined by merely comparing the resulting increases and decreases in tariffs required to reach
the calculated level. For a producer within the Community that was
previously protected by a high tariff, the most serious challenge to its
competitive position will come from low cost producers *within* the
Community against which it will have no tariff protection. Unless
the high cost producers can bring their prices (and costs) down to
the level of the low cost producers within the EEC, then they cannot
stay in business. The essence of economic integration depends on
this type of competition taking place. The prices of the large, low-
cost producers within the Community will set the competitive level
for the entire market. The common external tariff will be protective
only to the extent that it protects the firms that can compete success-
fully within the market. . . .

The impact of these higher EEC tariffs upon United States
exports may well be substantial. . . . Up to now, the United States has
benefited greatly from the rapid growth of the European economies
and the pressures put on the German engineering industry in particular. We have been the residual supplier making the most of excess
demand. However, this may not continue.

If Great Britain should join the Common Market, further difficulties will be created for American exports. As desirable as the union
may be on other grounds, it will cause a twofold increase in the
troubles facing U. S. exporters. In the first place, as British exports
cease to feel the discrimination of the EEC, an easy target for market
dislodgment by the EEC and U. S. producers will be removed.
Furthermore, the British themselves then may well become a serious
competitor for existing American shares of the EEC market. In all
the twenty-two product groups in which U. S. exports are concentrated, with the exception of paper and paperboard, the British also
have a substantial position. In seven groups, the British share of the
EEC market exceeds our own, and it is well above 5 percent for most
of the others. This means that the British have a substantial base
for expanding their exports if their competitive position improves.
The competitive pressures arising from membership in the EEC and
the tariff preferences gained thereby may be enough to transform the
British into a fierce competitor. United States exports would become
the prime target under such circumstances and maintaining our
market position in industrial products would not be easy.

U. S. AGRICULTURAL EXPORTS TO THE EUROPEAN
ECONOMIC COMMUNITY[4]

The most serious challenge to United States exports arises from the adoption this year by the EEC of a common agricultural policy. While many important aspects of the policy are yet to be determined, the major impact of the policy can be inferred from the mechanism that has been created. This development is of particular concern to the United States because Western Europe is such a large purchaser of U. S. agricultural products. During recent years the EEC countries alone absorbed over 20% of our agricultural exports and close to one-third of all such exports sold for hard currencies. The addition of the U. K. to the Common Market would increase the latter percentage to one-half and amounts to $1.5 billion.

The agricultural agreement of January 14, 1962, provides the initial steps for the integration of the agricultural sector of the EEC. The regulations found in the agreement differ substantially among the various products, but there are some common features. Existing restrictions of all kinds on imports are to be replaced by variable levies designed to offset the differences in market prices (after adjusting for transportation costs) in the EEC country importing and in the country of origin. The levies on imports from other EEC countries are to be gradually reduced until 1970, when a one-price system will emerge. The levies on imports from non-EEC countries are to be sufficiently high to ensure preference for imports from other EEC countries; they will not be reduced over time and might be increased if Community and world prices diverge further.

This system of variable levies will work in such a way that a chain of preference will be set up. Demands for agricultural products in any EEC country will be met first by domestic production. Should these supplies prove insufficient at existing support prices, then products from other EEC countries will be allowed into the market. Only if aggregate production within the Community is insufficient will imports be allowed from non-EEC countries, regardless of how competitively priced these goods may be.

Provision is also made in the agreement for export subsidies designed to offset differences in market prices which will enable a member country with an exportable surplus to export to another

[4] A more extensive treatment of this subject can be found in my paper published by the Joint Economic Committee, *Factors Affecting the United States Balance of Payments,* Part 2, The Common Market: New Challenges to U.S. Exports, 1962.

member country needing imports but having a lower price level. Subsidies on intra-Community trade will disappear by 1970. However, similar provisions are made for export subsidies in the event that the Community as a whole experiences an exportable surplus to enable its products to compete in world markets and these provisions will not end with the transition period.

With imports determined solely as a residual between production and consumption of agricultural products within the Common Market, evaluation of the consequences of this policy depends on these magnitudes. Since the target level of price supports has not yet been agreed upon (nor pricing criteria), production cannot be estimated with certainty. The eventual agreement on price level will result from a compromise of the political requirements within the member countries. So far the West Germans have been particularly unwilling to consider a lowering of their price supports and German prices are the highest in the Community. In all likelihood, agreement can only be reached by substantially raising the average level of prices within the Community.

The implications for EEC imports of agricultural products from nonmember countries are quite clear. With rising average prices, increases in production will exceed increases in consumption and an accelerated movement toward self sufficiency for a wide range of products will occur. U. S. exports of wheat, coarse grains and meat will be endangered and these products make up a substantial portion of our exports. Some other U. S. exports will be undermined by the granting of tariff preferences to the products of the Associated Overseas Countries: namely, fats and oils and to a lesser extent tobacco and cotton.

Even with this overall pessimistic expectation, the United States will probably fare better than most third country exporters of agricultural products because of the structure of our comparative advantage. The U. S. exports mainly coarse grains to Europe rather than wheat, poultry rather than beef or lamb, and oil seeds, cotton and tobacco rather than cocoa, coffee and sugar. The prospects are that other countries whose product structure is concentrated in the latter categories will be in a much worse position than the U. S.

The aggregate of unfortunate consequences for nonmember countries of the common agricultural policy is greater than the sum of the losses in individual product markets. The agreement essentially removes the agricultural sector of the EEC from the resource allocating mechanism of world-market forces. If the EEC policy is pursued without moderation, bargaining for trade liberalization will be almost impossible because the mechanism ensures an absolute level of protection.

EXPORTS OF NON-AGRICULTURAL RAW MATERIALS

While the United States exports a considerable amount of nonagricultural crude materials to the Common Market ($750 million in 1960), the common external tariff is unlikely to interfere very greatly with this trade. Only for two commodity groups, petroleum products and aluminum, is the United States likely to suffer a trade loss. The loss may arise from the expansion of capacity that is induced by the tariff shelter. For most other products in this category, the external tariff is either zero or very low.

TRADE EFFECTS OF THE EEC VIA THIRD COUNTRIES

The commerce of the United States can be further affected by the Common Market even though American goods are not directly involved. If countries which normally spend a substantial portion of their foreign exchange earnings in the United States have their exports curtailed, then our balance of payments will subsequently suffer. This may well come about through tariff preferences granted the Associated Overseas Countries by the EEC.

The former French colonial areas of Africa are already substantial exporters of most tropical zone agricultural products, and these compete with Latin American exports to Europe. The common external tariff levied on Latin American goods plus the marketing privileges offered African products gives a distinct competitive edge to the African suppliers. If there were a net shortage or balance of world supplies relative to demand at ruling prices, then the diversion of African supplies to Europe would leave other markets open to Latin America. Since, however, there are more than sufficient world supplies of coffee, cocoa, sugar, and tropical fruit (the principal products involved), the losses to Latin America of sales to Europe as a result of tariff discrimination cannot be made up elsewhere and are likely to lead to a substantial loss in foreign exchange for the Latin Americans. Since the Latin American countries buy from 48% to 64% of their total imports from the United States while the African countries buy only 4% of the total imports from us, the net loss to United States exports from the preferential position which the EEC affords African supplies could be substantial.

A further problem is created for the United States because

another good customer of ours, Japan, is prevented from exporting to the EEC. All of the member countries discriminate against Japanese goods either by refusing to grant most-favored-nations treatment or by more devious methods. This affects us in two ways. The Japanese are denied foreign exchange, a major part of which would have been spent in the United States, and the Japanese are forced to send a disproportionate share of their output to the U. S. because we have the only market that is even partially open to them. The problem promises to be more serious as Japanese development continues. Even though discriminations against the Japanese predate the Rome Treaty, they are aggravated by the EEC because the freedom of transhipment of goods within the EEC will limit the liberalization of their restrictions to the pace of the least liberal country. Since the EEC countries must liberalize jointly, the speed of the liberalization measures will be much slower than the pace some countries were prepared to undertake in its absence.

OFFSET: HIGHER RATES OF GROWTH OF THE EEC COUNTRIES

In discussions of the external impact of economic integration, the point is always made that the unfavorable impact of the formation of a customs union on nonmember country exports will be offset in whole or in part by the increase in member country growth rates stimulated by the establishment of internal free trade. If the EEC has had, or is likely to have, a growth-stimulating effect, then it must be recognized that the beneficial consequences of this growth on the trade positions on nonmember countries is not as great as one might expect at first glance. Since this growth is likely to be of an import-replacing character, the natural consequences of stimulating growth via exports induced by preferential tariffs, the quantity of additional imports demanded from nonmember countries is likely to be less per unit of growth in income than could have been expected from past behavior. It is not enough for the growth of income merely to lead to a slight increase in imports from nonmembers if the Community's extra exports to the rest of the world per unit of growth of income are not declining sufficiently fast to maintain balance.

In order to make the point somewhat differently, consider the EEC as if it were a single country. The character of the growth of this country is such that it is progressively requiring less imports per unit of output. If at the same time, the exports of the country are not also declining fast enough in relation to GNP, then other countries' balances of payments will be put under pressure. Merely to maintain the existing balance-of-payments positions of third countries, outsiders will have to improve their competitive position vis-a-vis the Common Market. Rapid growth within the EEC has not so far led to a deterioration in their competitive positions in third markets; in fact, the contrary may be true. As a result, rapid growth of the EEC has been combined with balance of payments surpluses.

SUMMARY AND CONCLUSIONS

As indicated previously, the consequences of the Common Market for nonmember countries will depend as much or more on subsequent policy decisions of the Community as on the provisions of the Rome Treaty. This analysis suggests that at present nonmember countries have been put in a disadvantageous position. Future developments will depend in large measure on the willingness of the EEC to recognize the interests of nonmembers in their deliberations or, to use the standard phraseology, whether the Common Market will be outward or inward looking. There is some evidence to indicate that up to now the Community has been looking a little in both directions.

One can get some comfort in the belief that the Common Market will be outward looking from the Rome Treaty itself. Article 110 indicates that the interests of the Community lie in expanding world trade. Furthermore the influential leaders of the Commission of the EEC and Professor Hallstein in particular have continually supported this belief in public statements. Nor has the liberalism of the Common Market been confined to words alone. The first two internal tariff reductions were generalized to nonmember countries (as long as the resulting tariff did not fall below the external target rate). Also the Common Market was willing to enter negotiations through GATT in the so-called "Dillon round" and eventually reached agreements with other countries through which their external tariff was reduced by almost 20%.

There is some indication, however, of less liberal tendencies within the EEC. The tariff reductions made so far by the Common Market have been relatively painless in that they have merely removed some but not most of the excess protection created by the common external tariff. The common agricultural policy, however, has not only raised *new* barriers to trade, it has established a system that guarantees perfect protection. This policy can only be considered as a punitive measure from the point of view of agricultural exporting countries.

Policy formation within the Common Market, of course, is not created in a vacuum. If the United States moves toward greater trade restrictions through actions such as raising tariffs on carpets and glass, then we strengthen the protectionist forces within the EEC and bring forth retaliatory restrictions to an excessive degree such as did occur. With the passage of the Trade Expansion Act, the United States has taken the first step toward leadership in the liberal direction. It is now up to the Common Market to indicate its willingness to proceed along this road.

Unfortunately the immediate response in Europe to the American overture seems far from enthusiastic. While there is little question as to the willingness of the EEC to take part in another tariff negotiation, the hoped-for major reduction in tariffs that is possible under the American law has little chance of acceptance according to some EEC spokesmen.[5] If a negotiated tariff reduction seems difficult, then a unilateral reduction by the EEC of their tariffs seems remote indeed. Yet according to this analysis, a unilateral reduction by the EEC is called for to satisfy the spirit, if not the letter, of the GATT requirement that protection not be increased through the formation of a customs union.

The economic size and power of the European Economic Community has cast it in a leadership role in the world. This power, unfortunately, can be used to further the narrow self interest of the member countries as they conceive it to be. A continuance of existing political institutions almost assures that the power will be used in this way. On the other hand, responsible exercise of this power is possible with the development of greater political unity. Many difficult decisions would have to be made in exercising enlightened leadership, such as inducing major shifts of resources out of agriculture, and this is possible only with a strong sense of unity among the members.

Political unity may but need not mean a single federal state. Certainly many transitional stages would be gone through even if a single state was the ultimate goal. Fortunately responsible leadership need not depend on reaching this particular ideal of unity. Progress toward majority rule and closer coordination of national policies may well be sufficient. From this point of view, the accession of Great Britain to the Rome Treaty would be the most important single step toward bringing about a more outward looking Community. British membership would add greater balance to the Community and would assure members and nonmembers alike as to the permanence of European unity and thus responsibility would follow.

[5] Speech by M. Couve de Murville on February 20, 1962, before the American Club of Paris; speech by Valery Giscard d'Estaing on March 27, 1962, at the opening of the Lyon Trade Fair; and speech by Michel Maurice Bokanowski on October 25, 1962, to the American Chamber of Commerce in Paris.

DAVID E. BELL

Foreign Aid and the
Balance of Payments*

As ADMINISTRATOR of the Agency for International Development, I am particularly pleased that these hearings are being held, for they present an excellent opportunity to give the facts to the Congress and to attempt to clear up some of the misconceptions surrounding the relation of aid to our balance of payments.

Foreign aid is by its very nature closely involved with the flow of payments. Thus each action and step taken by AID is and must be evaluated from the point of view of our balance-of-payments situation.

The foreign aid program provides goods and services to other countries which they cannot obtain through normal means — through their export earnings and through obtaining capital on commercial terms and by private investment. A successful aid program is one which enables the recipient country to strengthen its economy to the point where it can obtain goods and services it needs for steady expansion and growth by normal trade and normal capital movements — and without further need for aid grants and soft loans. This is what was achieved in Western Europe under the Marshall plan, and has since been achieved in Japan, Spain, Greece, Taiwan, and other countries.

It is plainly important to seek to carry out this important national program, like any other, at minimum cost to the United States.

In the first years of the U.S. foreign aid program after World War II, during the Marshall plan and most of the 1950's, our aid appropriations were, in general, spent wherever in the world prices were lowest. During the Marshall plan period, of course, the United States was the only major source in the world for most of the goods those countries needed. Therefore most of the aid dollars, although not tied to U.S. procurement, were spent in this country. Later in the 1950's the revived European economies became increasingly effective competitors for U.S. aid purchases.

* From a statement given before the U.S. Senate Banking and Currency Subcommittee in *Balance of Payments, 1965*, pp. 67–73.

Beginning in 1959, in response to the changed situation of the U.S. balance of payments, our policy respecting aid purchases was changed. Today, with small exceptions, aid appropriations can only be spent in the United States for goods and services produced in this country. This has undoubtedly raised the cost to the Federal budget of providing a given amount of goods and services under the aid program, since some items are being purchased with aid appropriations in the United States which could be bought more cheaply in other countries. But our present policies are intended to minimize the adverse effect of the aid program on the balance of payments, even if that results in some increased cost to the budget.

There are two approaches to measuring the impact of AID's expenditures on the balance of payments. The first, which might be called the "accounting" approach, measures the direct result of the AID spending: Are the dollars appropriated by the Congress spent directly in this country, or are they spent abroad or transferred to another country or to an international organization?

Under this method of measurement, which is similar to the Department of Commerce figures on the balance of payments, during fiscal year 1964 — the latest data available — the gross adverse effect on the U.S. balance of payments of AID's economic assistance programs was about $513 million.

We have now received preliminary estimates for the calendar year 1964 which show substantial further improvement. The payments abroad dropped to about $400 million. This is offset by repayments of past assistance extended by AID and predecessor agencies of over $150 million, making a net effect of about $250 million in the last calendar year.

The current expenditure rate under our economic assistance program is almost exactly $2 billion per year. Thus, in 1964, for every dollar of economic aid extended, 20 cents showed as a current adverse impact in our balance of payments — not considering current or future receipts.

Put the other way around, 80 percent of AID's expenditures last year represented not dollars going abroad, but steel, machinery, fertilizer, and other goods and services purchased in the United States.

Under these circumstances, of course, a cut in AID appropriations would primarily reduce U.S. exports, and would have only a very small effect on the balance of payments.

Moreover, the proportion of appropriations spent in the United

States is rising. Eighty-five per cent of new obligations are being committed for direct expenditure in the United States.

The $400 million of AID offshore payments in calendar 1964 is made up of the following major elements:

$120 million representing payments of the U.S. voluntary contributions to international organizations, such as U.N. agencies, the Indus River project administered by the IBRD, and the Social Progress Trust Fund.

$78 million for commodity purchases in other less-developed countries — cases where, for example, required goods are unavailable in the United States or shipping costs are too high.

$19 million for commodity purchases in other developed countries. These are either tag-end expenditures of major projects approved before aid was tied in 1959 or items unavailable from any other source, and they are all approved on a case-by-case waiver basis.

$66 million in cash transfers; a transfer of funds made in a very few cases where normal procedures for providing assistance are not feasible or made in small amounts to cover local costs of technical assistance projects. The amount of such transfers has been reduced sharply in recent years and is expected to be only $40 million in calendar year 1965.

$30 million for local expenses of AID direct-hire personnel stationed abroad. This represents the local expenses which could not be met by use of Treasury-owned local currencies.

$87 million for other expenditures outside the United States. This includes payments by U.S. contractors for such necessary items as wages. It also includes payments to schools and hospitals abroad, disaster relief expenditures, offshore expenses of participants, and other project costs.

As indicated above, this $400 million was offset by about $150 million in repayments of principal and interest on loans extended by AID and its predecessor agencies.

This then is the "accounting" measure of the direct flow of dollars abroad resulting from our economic aid program.

The true net economic effect of foreign assistance on our balance of payments cannot be measured so simply. This is because there are indirect effects not revealed by the direct accounts.

A substantial portion of the dollars that go out under our aid program, to the United Nations, for example, comes back through regular commercial channels for purchases of U.S. goods.

Dollars which go out and enter the economy of a less developed country may be used later by that country to buy needed goods in the U.S. market, or may go through trade channels to a third country, which will use the dollars for purchase of goods in the U.S. market.

These are examples of the so-called feedback effect, which means that the effect of aid outflows on the U.S. balance of payments is overstated, because dollar outflows to a considerable extent are immediately reflected in increased U.S. export sales for dollars.

But there is another indirect effect in the opposite direction. When an aid recipient is able to buy U.S. imports under a tied loan — that is, has a letter of credit opened in a U.S. bank which can only be spent in the United States — then that country may use the tied dollars to buy goods that it would have otherwise bought with dollars it already owns.

These other dollars — free exchange — are thus available for other purchases either in the United States or elsewhere. This is the so-called substitution effect, meaning that to some extent aid-financed imports are "substituted" for imports that would have been bought with "free" dollars, and to this extent the effect of tied aid on the U.S. balance of payments is understated.

There are no good estimates of the size of the feedback aid substitution effects. Only indirect evidence is available. With respect to the question of how much substitution occurs, for example, it is clear that most of the less-developed countries have severe shortages of dollars, and need more goods from the United States than they can afford, even with the addition of aid. Furthermore, statistics do not indicate that a dropoff in commercial trade occurs when there is an increase in aid. Quite the opposite.

The most frequently cited example is Latin America. While expenditures under the Alliance for Progress have been increasing over the last 3 years, so have Latin American purchases from the United States through regular commercial channels. In fact, according to preliminary estimates, commercial U.S. exports to Latin America increased by $500 million in 1964 alone.

Thus it is the best guess of the economists who have studied these matters that the amount of substitution is relatively small.

Overall, it is our conclusion that the indirect economic effects of aid on our balance of payments roughly balance each other, and even allowing for some variation from time to time, the true effect of aid on our balance of payments would not differ very much in either direction from the figures shown by the accounting estimates referred to earlier.

To sum up, our balance-of-payments figures show, by the

"accounting" measure, the share of our expenditures made directly for U.S. goods and services is 80 percent and rising, and the share paid to the foreigners and international organizations is 20 percent and falling.

These figures do not take into account indirect effects, but it is our best guess that they would be little different if they did. AID dollars spent abroad which return quickly in payment for commercial exports roughly offset the amount of AID financing for goods that would have been exported anyway. As nearly as we can tell these two imperfections roughly cancel each other out and 15–20 percent is a valid indication of the real adverse impact of aid on the U.S. balance of payments.

I should like to say a word about the relationship of U.S. aid and holdings of U.S. gold.

Some aid recipients have bought gold from the United States in the past few years, mostly to finance their gold subscriptions to the International Monetary Fund. . . .

In the main, however, gold transactions between the United States and aid recipients result in a net gain in U.S. holdings. During 1964, for example, less developed countries purchased $26 million worth of gold from the United States, of which all but $3 million was subscribed to the IMF, but they sold $89 million worth of gold to us for dollars in the same period.

Thus, there is no direct relation between aid and an outflow of gold to aid recipients. In fact, the reverse is true. The U.S. gold problem lies with the industrial countries of Europe, not in our relations with the aid-recipient nations.

I have been speaking thus far of AID expenditures. There are other U.S. programs which can properly be referred to as foreign aid in a broad sense. I should like to mention these briefly, with a word about their balance-of-payments impact.

Military assistance consists principally of the provision of U.S. produced military equipment. Taking into account the cost of U.S. personnel overseas to administer the program, some oversea training costs, and other oversea expenditures, the estimates are that over 85 percent of military assistance expenditures are made directly in the United States and the remainder are made offshore.

The Public Law 480 program provides U.S. surplus agricultural commodities by sale and donation to other countries. In view of the nature of the program, virtually all of the expenditures under it are made directly in the United States, with only minor and unavoidable offshore costs in foreign ports. The same is true of expenditures under the Export-Import Bank loans.

The Peace Corps expenditures are almost entirely for the living expenses of the volunteers abroad, and for their training and supervision in the United States. It is estimated that about 75 percent of Peace Corps expenditures are made in the United States, and about 25 percent offshore.

Finally, U. S. contributions to international agencies, such as the International Development Association, are paid in dollars and are shown in the Department of Commerce statistics as 100-percent outflows. In fact, however, a substantial share of the total expenditures of these international organizations is made in the United States. Consequently, the accounting estimate of balance-of-payments impact in this case overstates the true effect.

I should like to stress that we are seeking in every way we can to use local currencies, owned by the United States as a result of food-for-peace sales or other U.S. assistance, to meet the local costs of our aid missions.

The net effect of this policy is to enable us in many countries to substitute U.S.-produced commodities for what would otherwise be dollars used to purchase local currencies to cover the local costs of U.S. Government activities.

President Johnson's message of February 10 said:

Until we master our balance-of-payments problem AID officials will send no aid dollars abroad that can be sent instead in the form of U.S. goods and services.

We are doing just that. I have asked that every project and every commodity order be closely examined. Waiver of tied procurement regulations will be allowed only when it is clearly justified in the U.S. interest. Local costs will be paid for out of U.S. local currency holdings wherever possible.

We expect, as I have indicated, to see some further increase in tied purchases and expenditures in the United States, but we are close to the limit. Some minimum offshore expenditures will remain — principally the local expenditures of our employees and those of our contractors who are stationed overseas, the contributions of the United States to international organizations, and a few special cases where tying to U.S. procurement is unfeasible or unwise.

The President, advised by this Cabinet Committee on the Balance of Payments, has concluded that this small remaining element of offshore expenditures under the aid program is a cost to our country which is far outweighed by the benefits to our own interests that will accrue from the achievement of economic and social progress in the less developed countries.

A similar judgment underlay the distinction drawn by the President in his recent balance-of-payments message between U.S. private investment abroad in advanced countries — which for the time being is to be discouraged — and U.S. private investment abroad in less developed countries, which the U.S. Government is continuing strongly to encourage.

Looking beyond the immediate present, the foreign aid program has a number of effects which are positively beneficial to our balance of payments.

First, our aid today is overwhelmingly in the form of dollar repayable loans — unlike the situation under the Marshall plan, when 90 per cent of our aid was in the form of grants.

Future repayments of interest and principal on today's loans will be a positive factor in our balance of payments.

Second, the evidence is plain that countries which with our aid achieve steady economic growth become increasingly better markets for U.S. exports and more attractive places for U.S. investment abroad.

Over the last 15 years our exports to Europe have doubled and our exports to Japan have tripled. As other countries — Spain, Greece, Taiwan, and so on — gain economic momentum and our aid comes to an end, the same kind of result is evident.

Moreover, the aid program in case after case has directly led to the introduction of American products and services in other countries, and to follow-on markets unrelated to the aid program. Aid has in fact been one of our best export promotion mechanisms.

In conclusion, Mr. Chairman, I am pleased to report that since 1961 we have steadily reduced the effect of foreign aid on our balance of payments. We are continuing these efforts to minimize the effect as part of the action program announced by President Johnson last month.

We will do more. But the upper limit may soon be reached, as the adverse impact has already been reduced to $400 million, not including repayments.

In addition, it is important to recognize that a continuation of the present program will have a long-range positive impact on our balance of payments as a result of a dollar repayment flow, expanding markets for our exports and improving opportunities for our private investment abroad. . . .

ECONOMIC AID AND THE BALANCE OF PAYMENTS

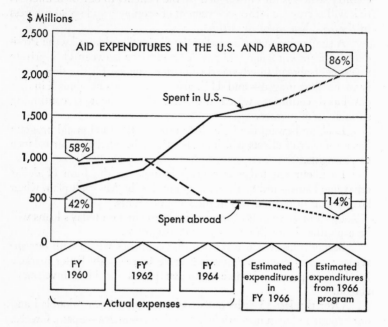

AID EXPENDITURES IN THE U.S. AND ABROAD

AID'S EFFECT ON DEFICIT IN U.S. BALANCE OF PAYMENTS

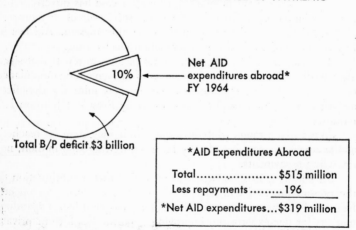

The Deficit: A Diagnosis*

It seems to us important, in an empirical analysis of the causes of the balance-of-payments deficit to establish: First, whether it is a short-term or a long-term problem; and second, whether current policies give promise of solving our problem.

Before we discuss the specific accounts of the U. S. balance of payments, Mr. Chairman, we would first like to break down our overall position into private and Government sectors. This is done in the attached table. . . . It is clear from even a cursory perusal of these data that our balance-of-payments deficit lies mainly in the Government sector. . . .

If we take the Government sector first, we can see that consistently throughout the 1960 to 1964 period, the expenditures exceeded the receipts by about $3 to $4 billion. We have excluded from the Government sector receipts through the sale of medium-term convertible securities, otherwise known as the Roosa bonds, and the prepayment of debt, which is really a way of borrowing from your future receipts. If they were included, the deficits in the Government sector would still run between $2 and $4 billion a year. So that it is obvious from the reviewing of these charts that the hard core of our deficit lies in the Government sector.

While it is true in a private sector there are certain areas where expenditures exceed receipts — namely, in the service part of the private sector, that is, tourism and transportation — our overall position has been in surplus export /since exports/ plus investment income certainly exceed imports, plus long-term capital investment, not only consistently, but in growing proportions throughout the period. Furthermore, it may be noted that part of these exports are through foreign affiliates of U. S. foreign investment enterprises. . . .

Mr. Chairman, I would like now to summarize the implications of these facts and make certain recommendations.

(1) It is a major error of fact to blame private capital exports, particularly direct investments abroad, for the balance of payments

* From a statement before the U.S. Senate Banking and Currency Subcommittee in *Balance of Payments, 1965,* pp. 471–473 and 498–503.

TABLE I — PRIVATE AND GOVERNMENT SECTORS IN THE U.S. BALANCE OF PAYMENTS, 1960–64

[In billions of dollars]

	1960–61 (average)		1962		1963		1964	
	Private	Government	Private	Government	Private	Government	Private	Government
Exports	17.6	2.1	18.1	3.0	19.3	3.4	22.4	3.6
Income on investments	3.2	.4	3.9	.5	4.0	.5	4.7	.5
Other service receipts	3.9	.2	4.1	.2	4.7	.2	5.1	.3
Long-term capital inflows	.4	....	.3	....	.3	....	.2	....
Repayments to U.S. Government[1]	....	.5	....	.6	....	.6	....	.6
Government liabilities[2]	....	.1	....	.9	....	.4	....	.4
Total receipts	+25.1	+3.3	+26.4	+5.2	+28.3	+5.1	+32.4	+5.4
Imports	−14.6	....	−16.1	....	−17.0	....	−18.6	....
Services	−5.2	−.9	−5.6	1.0	−6.2	−1.1	−6.5	−1.2
Private long-term investments	−2.6	....	−2.8	....	−3.5	....	−4.3	....
Military cash outflows	....	−3.0	....	−3.0	....	−2.9	....	−2.8
Government grants and loans	....	−3.8	....	−4.3	....	−4.5	....	−4.3
Total payments	−22.4	−7.7	−24.5	−8.3	−26.8	−8.5	−29.4	−8.3
Basic position	+2.8	−4.4	+1.9	−3.1	+1.5	−3.4	+3.0	−2.9
Short-term capital outflows:								
Increase in private short-term assets abroad	−1.4	....	−.5	....	−.7	....	−2.1	....
Unrecorded outflows	−.6	....	−1.0	....	−.3	....	−.9	....
Balance on regular transactions	+.8	−4.4	+.4	−3.1	+.5	−3.4	....	−2.9

[1] Excludes debt prepayments of $53,000,000 in 1960, $696,000,000 in 1961, $681,000,000 in 1962, $326,000,000 in 1963, and $115,000,000 during 1964.

[2] Excludes sale of medium-term Government securities to foreign governments which totaled $251,000,000 in 1962, $702,000,000 in 1963, and $375,000,000 in 1964.

Source: U.S. Department of Commerce, "Survey of Current Business," June 1964, pp. 10–11; December 1964, pp. 10–11, and March 1965, pp. 12, 14.

deficits. It is a major error in policy to try and resolve the deficits by control of private investments abroad, particularly in developed countries.

About $9 billions of foreign revenues — more than one-fourth of our total external earnings — are derived from direct private investments abroad. It makes no sense as a national policy to try and retard, discourage, or control, this source of external income.

The attempt to deal with deficits through the private capital account is also based on the assumption that the balance of payments deficit is a short-term phenomenon. Our analysis of the facts indicates that it is due to the continued $7 to $9 billion a year Government transfers of wealth and purchasing power abroad.

As long as this continues, the deficit will not be temporary but a permanent phenomenon, and we should exert all our efforts in earning money on investments from countries that are stable and secure in their political structure and currency.

This country cannot possibly meet its continuing obligations abroad by making it a habit of appropriating, year after year, billions of dollars for long-term, soft, no-interest loans and grants and military expenditures abroad, while at the same time curtailing one of the two most important sources of cash income, secure investments abroad.

(2) I think the facts indicate that it is also an illusion to think that we can solve this problem by expanding exports unilaterally while we curtail investments abroad.

The facts show that much of our favorable export accounts are in machinery and raw materials, mostly to developed countries, in part due to our direct investments. In other categories such as consumer end products, the trends have turned against us.

One of our easy assumptions is that we are competitive in the price of manufacturers. During my extensive travels abroad, one of the first explanations given by U.S. commercial counselors for the diminishing percentage of U.S. exports in relation to total imports of other countries is noncompetitiveness of American products in price.

Of course, there are items in which we are in a favorable position. But there are many products in which this is not true. Because our desire in the period after World War II was to encourage exports from the war-torn countries, we built certain biases into international agreements.

For example, the GATT agreement allows the forgiveness of turnover taxes in exports, it does not allow a similar concession of income taxes. As European countries base their tax system mainly on turnover taxes, this favors the European exporter to the extent of 20 or 25 percent in export price discounts, without being accused of dumping or export subsidies, but any move by us to forgive a portion of income taxes on exported goods would be considered in violation of GATT.

There is another structural development which will inhibit U.S. exports to an increasing degree. This is the growth of common markets and free trade areas, as well as the desire of developing countries to be self-sufficient in manufactures.

The very essense of common markets is to favor the members and discriminate against the nonmembers. Thus the prospects of increasing net earnings by exports of manufactured end products will be limited.

The permission to establish common markets and to discriminate against nonmembers, without violating the most-favored-nation provision of GATT is another provision established in the postwar period to favor Europe.

The opportunities of solving this problem by a unilateral increase in exports of $3 billion are not good. The underdeveloped countries do not have the cash — they want foreign aid which they will use for industrial development behind protective tariff walls.

The Communist countries are limited in their gold and foreign exchange resources, and the best you can hope for there is limited exports of essentials, such as grain, and barter arrangements; or long-term credits, which would not help our balance of payments.

Many of the developed countries, Japan, Canada, and Great Britain, have their own balance of payments deficits, and hence, are in no position to increase imports from us unilaterally. In fact, all three of these countries are trying to reduce their deficits by buying less abroad and selling more.

This leaves us with the surplus countries, mostly the EEC and Spain. It would require almost a 100 percent increase in our sales to them to increase our exports by $3 billion; or we would have to take away that much of their markets in third countries — both attempts fraught with both economic and political dangers.

Thus, we have been pursuing a national policy since 1961 which was contrary to recognizable historical trends, could not possibly have succeeded, and, by following an illusion, we have delayed other solutions of the problem of our deficits.

(3) The assumption that the trade negotiations under the Kennedy Round will help us improve our balance of payments position needs much more careful scrutiny than it has received to date.

The Common Market's desire is to lower our tariffs in categories of industries and products which heretofore have given us the largest trade account surplus. The very controversy on tariff disparities is designed to breach the U.S. market in those products.

On the other hand, in fields such as grain exports, where we have a tremendous price advantage, we have made concessions in the Dillion Round of negotiations in order to help the completion of the Common Market arrangements: in accepting the variable levies and a high price support program in the EEC, both of which threaten to diminish our exports of these products.

In the area of consumer end products, I am afraid the statistical trends show the prospects of our increasing cash sales are rather dim.

Everybody seems to want our machinery for tooling up to produce their own consumer products, and it is doubtful that the current trade negotiations will change that trend. Whenever there is an opportunity to increase sales, as for instance in U.S. compact cars, the nontariff barriers put in our way are insurmountable and possibly beyond the reach of trade negotiations.

(4) It is a current illusion that tied aid prevents leakage of dollars. A more careful and penetrating analysis of aid and trade will indicate, I believe, that more and more of our sales to underdeveloped countries are being shifted from cash account to credit account, and the saving in dollar exchange resulting therefrom is being spent in other countries. This is true also of the aid given by international institutions.

(5) In the area of defense expenditures abroad, there has perhaps been some lag also in appreciating the significance of new technological developments. This lag is perhaps responsible for the maintenance of troops in Western Europe 20 years after the termination of hostilities.

We are not, of course, in a position to make recommendations with respect to strategic military planning, but one cannot help but wonder whether there are not some alternative arrangements or choices we can offer to our allies that will diminish our out-of-pocket expenses for this purpose.

RECOMMENDATIONS

With these conclusions in mind, we would like to advance for your consideration a number of specific recommendations.

(1) We should stop frightening the capital markets of the world by hints of forthcoming controls and regulations. There is nothing more sensitive in economic life than liquid capital.

We must remember that, in addition to such capital held by institutions and individuals of other nations and U.S. corporations, there are millions and millions of Americans with money in the bank who may be scared into taking panic action that will bring about the very consequences we seek to avoid. We should stop frightening capital into unnecessary movements.

(2) A very determined effort should be made, in addition to those already undertaken by the Defense Department and AID, to curtail Government outlays abroad by approximately $1 billion.

To accomplish this, we suggest, first, converting the foreign aid program to a lend-lease basis instead of a line-of-credit basis, financing only U.S.-procured components of specific incremental development projects. This means termination of program loans, balance-of-payments loans and budgetary assistance.

The present techniques of giving foreign aid have proved wasteful, because they finance current consumption and unproductive employment; and have added to our balance-of-payments deficits because they cause substitution of credit sales for cash sales.

Where there is absolute military necessity for balance-of-payments and budgetary help, then the President should be provided with sufficient contingency funds to take care of it on a case-by-case basis.

At the same time, more discriminating attention should be given to opportunities for dollar sales under title IV of Public Law 480, and for a possible amendment to title I, which would require at least 25 percent payment in hard currency.

It would indeed help our balance of payments much more if we got 25 percent in dollars or other hard currencies, and made a gift of the rest, than to maintain the illusion of cash sales for local currencies.

While these changes are being worked out, we recommend at lease a 20-percent cut in section 202 and 252 appropriations under the Foreign Assistance Act, immediately, and that they be phased out completely as soon as the lend-lease program is set up.

(3) The United States should become more aggressive in the protection of existing markets in our trade negotiations. To accomplish this, we must cease putting undefinable political objectives ahead of clearly definable economic advantages. . . .

(4) Immediate steps should be taken by Export-Import Bank (a) to stop making balance-of-payments loans as an adjunct of AID policy, and return to its original purpose of making specific project loans to encourage exports, and (b) to liberalize its export credit and insurance facilities to become completely competitive with similar facilities offered by other countries.

(5) We should put the Common Market countries on notice that the United States will take steps to reduce its military expenses and

tourist expenses in the balance-of-payments surplus countries by at least $1 billion unless they make an offer to purchase, additionally, from us at least that amount of incremental products by reducing their protectionist devices against the U.S. agricultural products for which they have need and which we can provide at reasonable prices; and be prepared to carry it out.

Another alternative they should be offered is sharing in the costs of Western defense by an equivalent amount.

(6) The Congress should instruct the Executive to cease and desist from further commitments to international institutions for foreign aid, until prior authorization is obtained from the Congress. I think we should put a moratorium for a whole on appropriations for no-interest, long-term, soft loans.

The Congress should also instruct, by legislation, our representatives in these institutions, particularly the World Bank and the Inter-American Bank, to vote against the issuance of bonds in the U.S. market, and insist that dollar loans be tied to U.S. procurement.

It is not easy to understand how, consistently, the Congress can tell foreign borrowers not to come to the American money market and American investors to refrain from investing abroad, while these international institutions, with the faith and credit of the U.S. Government behind them, borrow in the United States, get generous appropriations, and lend untied funds to underdeveloped countries.

(7) The U.S. Government should take a good hard look at the effect of international commodity agreements on U.S. balance of payments. Are international cartels, even if contrived by governments, the effect of which is to raise the price of imports, in the U.S. interest? Are commodity agreements, such as the wheat agreement, the effect of which is to share markets, rather than sell more U.S. agricultural production, to the interest of our country? Are international price maintenance subsidies, as in sugar, to the interest of the United States? Can we not devise ways whereby, if the U.S. consumer is called upon to pay a premium price, the difference between world price and U.S. price can be set aside as a foreign aid fund, thereby diminishing the necessity of direct aid appropriations?

Again, in this area, the United States faces the responsibility of developing a policy consistent with our overall commitments and interests.

(8) The charters of the post-World War II international institutions should be reexamined to see whether they need amendments to bring them in line with current conditions. Established at a time when the world bias was in favor of Europe, many of these provisions

now prevent the United States from taking initiatives in solving current problems.

I have already referred to two provisions of GATT, in tax treatment, and in exceptions given to EEC, which make it difficult for us to expand our exports. There are other institutions, such as the World Bank, IDA, Inter-American Bank, which need to be reviewed. This reexamination should include the proportion of U.S. participation, procurement policies, and the purposes for which funds are to be used.

Every 2 years the Congress is presented with proposed amendments, always for increased appropriations, but never with any substantive changes in charter provisions.

The next revision should concern itself with fundamental amendments of the charters of these institutions. But before going into such an effort, it is to be hoped that the Congress will find ways of studying these charters and making basic recommendations to the Executive.

I wish to thank the committee for its patience and indulgence in hearing out our extensive examination. We have devoted a great deal of time and effort in studying these problems. It is extremely heartening to us that such an important body as this committee has made this effort worthwhile by giving us this opportunity.

I must also express my personal gratitude and pleasure to our member companies which have given us the freedom to speak out the truth as we see it. The points we have made here are the results of research and discussions of the participants here. No one else has seen or reviewed this statement, not even committees of our organization or member companies.

I do not know whether they would agree or disagree with these conclusions and recommendations. Therefore, in all fairness, I want to save them any blame, and assume full responsibility for this presentation.

PART THREE

ALTERNATIVE CURES FOR THE DEFICIT

INTRODUCTION

The basic cause of the dollar deficit would seem to be a mixture of the adverse effects of decreased competitiveness in certain sectors; of reduced growth rates in some sectors of the world which normally buy large proportions of their imports from the United States; of stimulated outflows of long-term capital; of increased governmental overseas commitments; of a return to normalcy after a long period in which Western European nations were emphasizing recovery rather than aggressive exporting, and of the formation of the two trade blocs in Western Europe. All of these ingredients notwithstanding, one point cannot be too often emphasized: the dollar deficit is a market-flow concept and, by virtue of its consistent surpluses on current account, the United States has been increasing its holdings of foreign assets at a rate considerably in excess of the absolute rate of increase of its liabilities to foreigners. The root problem is then one of liquidity, not of net worth—the United States dollar is in deficit, not because the country has been living (consuming) beyond its income, but because it has been investing beyond its net saving (earnings less consumption).

However, the United States has taken deliberate policy measures to increase its net saving by reducing its consumption. Thus, the United States has borne (or rather the marginal workers have borne) higher rates of unemployment than official policy goals call for; not unrelated is the mediocre rate of growth achieved for the first few years of the awareness of the deficit. Harry G. Johnson adduces as evidence of lack of concern with the performance of the economy a whole series of individual measures taken to reduce the deficit. For Johnson, the combination of inadequate domestic performance and deficits argues that depreciation of the dollar in terms of other currencies, is the correct cure. Some of the measures detailed by Johnson are simply measures designed to depreciate the dollar in certain sectors, since a tariff on imports tends to increase U.S. competitiveness in the relevant market and is equivalent to a depreciation in that market. Johnson argues that such sectoral "depreciations" are bad policy. Since Johnson wrote his paper, the administration and economists have conceived several similar ideas, and some of these have been implemented. The idea of curbing foreign travel has been a happy hunting ground for such schemes: reductions of the duty-free exemptions for returning travelers have twice been effected and the concept of an export-visa tax, sent up as a trial balloon, was killed by a tidal wave of public opposition. In his assessment of the *1965 Economic Report of the President,* John Kenneth Galbraith conceived of the idea of a percentage tax on the pensions and dividends of wealthy expatriates.

Despite the good case for depreciation or devaluation which Johnson makes, Robert Z. Alibur and Galbraith both make equally, if not more, effective cases against it. In spite of the strength of the case for devaluation, it remains doubtful that a reduction in the value of the dollar relative to other currencies could, in fact, be achieved. If the United States were to reduce the value of the dollar in terms of gold, almost every other currency would simultaneously (or virtually so) undergo an equiproportionate reduction. Depreciation may not be a feasible policy alternative. In fact, the administration has repeatedly vowed to defend the exchange rate of the dollar regardless of the cost: depreciation is therefore not among the set of considered alternative policies.

Any proposals designed to change the relative values of national currencies have, as their ultimate goal, a reduction in the prices of United States goods and services relative to foreign goods and services. Depreciation of the dollar might be expected to have its greatest effect on current account transactions. Maintaining the existing prices of United States goods and services while foreign prices increase over time will achieve the same result of making United States goods relatively cheaper. This method of adjustment has been used as American prices showed great stability up to mid-1965 while European prices were advancing rapidly.

The crucial problem of the dollar seems to be that the market for dollars is concerned with current or short-run demand and supply. The market takes little or no account of the long-run strength of the dollar which the accumulation of foreign assets by U.S. residents argues. The problem is one of a nation in international imbalance being unable to implement or accept the necessary cure. The problem of "investing beyond net saving" is not new; it was a perennial problem for the Bank of England in the nineteenth century. Then, the dominance of London, the relative lack of concern of national governments for unemployment, perhaps greater sensitivities of both short and long-term capital to the cost of borrowing, and less price rigidity, all helped the traditional gold standard preserve international balance. However, modern society will no longer accept the traditional restraint of high interest rates and their consequences to reduce the volume of net exports of capital and to increase the surplus on current account. Instead of fairly violent short-run changes, the world now seeks to balance international accounts without imposing costs of unemployment and domestic price deflation.

One solution to the problem is an increased supply of world liquidity, which would enable nations to make slower and less painful adjustments to correct the causes of international imbalance. This concept would enable a nation to borrow larger amounts of internationally-acceptable credit so that the period of adjustment could be longer than that permitted by a "normal" stock of cash balances. The Brookings Report examines this type of solution and finds it to be the most desirable resolution of the dollar deficit. This belief is based upon an estimate of the dollar deficit in 1968, which suggests that payments will be in balance by that time and that the trend will be a strengthening of the dollar. The original argument for increased international liquidity, however, was not concerned with the United States deficit or surplus but rather with a long-run difference between the rate of growth of the world's monetary gold stock and the greater rate of growth of the monetary value of the world's international trade. While an expansion of world liquidity would ease the short-term adjustments of individual nations and finance the greater volume of trade, it is important that the two problems be kept separate in the reader's mind. The need for increased liquidity will not have disappeared when the United States achieves a balance in its international accounts; nor must United States proposals for greater liquidity disappear at that time.

The last two selections deal with two different attempts to reduce the net balance on capital account. Both policies concern themselves with differentials between foreign and domestic rates of interest. The existence of significant domestic unemployment in the United States clearly requires, *ceteris paribus,* low rates of interest. However, low rates of interest within the United States lead domestic owners of funds to seek higher rates abroad and foreign borrowers to attempt to borrow in the United States. The optimal policy is not clear, but this particular problem does not have one important aspect: of all types of international transaction on capital account, this portfolio action probably has the smallest proportional feedback. Exports of short-term capital and exports of portfolio capital (either to foreign borrowers or by domestic purchasers of foreign stocks and bonds) probably give rise to no direct increase in the volume of commodity exports and, further, the indirect increase in exports following from an injection of money may well be negligible.

For this reason, the concept of the interest equilization tax is clearly an enlightened policy measure. It aimed at reducing portfolio outflows without impairing the flow of direct investment or of raising the interest rate to deter domestic investment. After an initial success, the interest equilization tax merely transferred a lot of foreign borrowings from the capital market to commercial banks and seemed to lose its effectiveness. Recently, voluntary restraint on the part of commercial banks has reduced the rate of outflow of portfolio funds.

Finally, an attempt to attract short-term capital by raising the discount rate is assessed and found to be a costly means of financing a deficit.

HARRY G. JOHNSON

An Overview of Price Levels,
Employment, and the Balance
of Payments[*]

THE THEME of this paper is that the American economy is being
slowly crucified upon a cross of gold — gold inappropriately priced at
$35 an ounce.

The American economy has for six years been experiencing a
phase of mild economic stagnation, a phase which shows little sign of
terminating in the near future. Economic stagnation in this context
refers to two characteristics of economic performance — a higher
average rate of unemployment than previous experience has shown
to be necessary to the efficient operation of the economy, and a slower
rate of growth of productivity than either historical experience or
comparison with the contemporary record of other countries suggests
is attainable without economic strain. These two aspects of economic
stagnation are obviously interrelated in the case of the United States,
though the contrasting example of the United Kingdom, which until
the past year has experienced slow growth coupled with low unemployment rates, shows that the two do not always go together. . . . I
shall argue that the key to both aspects of American economic stagnation, and the source of the Administration's difficulties in overcoming it, is to be found still further back in the Keynesian tradition
than the *General Theory* — in the overvaluation of the currency to
which Keynes at one time attributed the stagnation of the British
economy in the interwar period.

I have followed the conventional wisdom in describing the
contemporary stagnation of the American economy as mild. It can
be described as mild only in the sense that unemployment has not
reached levels that constitute a threat to social and political stability,
and that growth has not been retarded to the extent of threatening a

* Reprinted from "An Overview of Price Levels, Employment, and the
Balance of Payments," by Harry G. Johnson in *The Journal of Business,* July
1963, pp. 279–289, by permission of the University of Chicago Press. Copyright 1964 by the University of Chicago.

revolution of frustrated aspirations of the kind that menaces a number of the underdeveloped countries. The loss of some $35 billion a year of potential output, and the unnecessary unemployment of some 2 per cent of the labor force, is not a trivial matter, even in a society aptly characterized as affluent. The stagnation of the past six years, and even more the prospect of continued stagnation in the years ahead, is on the contrary a serious problem for American economic policy for a host of reasons that extend far beyond the bounds of economics. Domestically, the image and the reality of America as a land where economic freedom results in increasing quality of opportunity and diminishing racial, religious, and social discrimination depends on the maintenance of high employment and rapidly rising output both to dissolve the uses of discrimination to protect privileged positions in the labor market, and to provide the resources necessary to support social arrangements aimed at correcting initial inequalities of birth and inheritance. Internationally, the powerful force of spreading industrialization has been steadily undermining the political, military, and economic leadership of the non-Communist world that the United States assumed after the war; economic stagnation in the United States both accelerates the undermining process and saps the capacity of the United States to sustain and exercise its leadership and to share it gracefully as other nations grow in strength. In addition, there is the danger that depressive influences radiating from the United States may drag the non-Communist world into a serious depression.

The economic stagnation of the United States has persisted, and threatens to persist into the future, in spite of the fact that the present Administration was elected in large part on the promise to "get the American economy moving again"; and that it has concentrated on the problems of economic policy more — and better — economic talent than has been employed by any previous Administration in the history of the United States. The inability of the Administration to deliver on its promises, in spite of its command over the services of the best brains of the economics profession, can be accounted for by one fundamental fact — the refusal of the governmental machinery in particular, and of public opinion in general, to face up to the root-source of the country's economic difficulties, the overvaluation of the dollar in relation to the major currencies of Europe. That refusal, which in turn is rooted in the mystery that envelops the whole subject of money in popular thinking and the mystique — carefully cultivated by practitioners — that surrounds the profession of central banking, necessarily obliges economic policy aimed at overcoming stagnation to direct its prescriptions at superficial symptoms and to concern itself with devising bits and pieces of economic gadgetry that at best can achieve inefficiently results that could be achieved more effectively and directly by policies aimed at the fundamental cause of the trouble.

The fact that the dollar is overvalued in relation to the European currencies, and has been so overvalued for an appreciable period, is indisputable. It is implicit, almost tautologically, in the fact that the country has been unable to achieve a satisfactory balance of payments, in spite of maintaining a higher level of unemployment than is generally considered desirable and in spite of the buttressing of the balance of payments by a variety of special measures designed to increase foreign-exchange receipts on both current and capital account beyond what would have resulted from normal commercial transactions. Objectively, the fact of overvaluation can be established by comparisons of relative purchasing powers of currencies or relative unit costs of production in different countries at existing exchange rates, as well as by more sophisticated econometric analysis of the exchange rate that would be consistent with international balance at full employment; the available statistical analyses suggest that the dollar is currently overvalued, by comparison with the major European currencies, by anywhere from 15 to 25 per cent.[1]

The existence and persistence of relative overvaluation of the dollar can be attributed to two features of postwar economic history. One was the prolongation of the process of European economic recovery, at least in its international aspects, manifest in the period of so-called chronic dollar shortage. Excess demand in Europe, and its concomitant of high demand for American goods, disguised the competitive advantage European industry acquired by the devaluations of 1949, and permitted and encouraged the inflationary upward trend of American wages and prices in the decade or so after the war. The desirability of a chronic American deficit of limited size as a means of increasing the international reserves of the European countries, and the temporary improvement of the American balance as a consequence of the Suez invasion, also served to conceal the growing competitive weakness of the United States in international markets.

---

[1] See Jaroslav Vanek, "Overvaluation of the Dollar: Causes, Effects, and Remedies," and H. S. Houthakker, "Exchange Rate Adjustment," both in Joint Economic Committee, Congress of the United States, *Factors Affecting the United States Balance of Payments: Compilation of Studies Prepared for the Sub-committee on International Exchange and Payments* (87th Cong., 2d sess. Washington, D.C.: Government Printing Office, 1962), pp. 267–304. . . .

The other feature was the hardening of the International Monetary Fund system, which was designed precisely to permit the correction of "fundamental disequilibrium" by changes in exchange rates, into a system of rigidly fixed exchange rates, in which the burden of adjustment is thrown on deflation by the deficit countries. The hardening process has been associated in part with the reassertion of the traditional morality of central banking, according to which inflation is an overriding evil to be prevented at all costs and, if experienced, to be atoned for by a confession of guilt in the form of a devaluation rather than relieved by appreciation of other currencies. The consequence of this system of morality is not only a marked reluctance to change exchange rates in either direction, but also a strong resistance to the alternative of adjusting domestic price levels to exchange rates on the part of the surplus countries, which are reluctant to allow domestic inflation to ease the improvident plight of the deficit countries, while the deficit countries are even more reluctant to effect adjustment by domestic deflation. In these circumstances, correction of disequilibrium is necessarily a slow and uncertain process, dependent on reluctant acceptance of abnormal unemployment to restrain wages and prices in the deficit countries, and reluctant yielding to inflationary pressures in the surplus countries; and the burden of it falls primarily on the deficit countries. The biasing of the burden toward the deficit countries would be mitigated, and the adjustment process accelerated, were it not for another factor also responsible for the hardening of the IMF system — the growing shortage of primary international reserves in the form of gold and the substitution for gold of holdings of convertible national currencies. The shortage of primary international reserves provides an additional reason for surplus countries to resist inflation, while the use of a national currency as an international reserve injects additional considerations of prestige and financial morality into the argument against devaluation.[2]

One other feature of postwar economic history deserves mention, not as a contributor to the existence and persistence of the overvaluation of the dollar but as a factor inhibiting the United States economic authorities from taking effective action to deal with the balance-of-payments problem and hence from remedying the associated problems of economic stagnation. This was the rapid assumption by the United States, under the joint pressures of the dollar shortage and the cold war, of the responsibilities of center country in the

[2] For a more extensive discussion of the international liquidity problem see Harry G. Johnson, "International Liquidity: Problems and Plans," *Malayan Economic Review*, VII, No. 1 (April 1962), 1–19.

international economy of the non-Communist world. During and immediately after the war it was fashionable among the economic critics of the United States to prophesy that the effort to restore a multilateral liberal international economic order would necessarily break down as a result of the unwillingness of the United States to take over from a senescent British economy the responsibilities of leader in liberal commercial policy, source of capital for the economic development of other less advanced nations, and center for the provision of banking and other financial services, that had knit the international economy into a functioning economic system in the nineteenth century, the division of which responsibilities among rival nations had been in large part responsible for the collapse of the liberal international order in the interwar period. In fact the United States shouldered these responsibilities with remarkable speed, at least from the long-run perspective of history. Although the assumption of the responsibility for the provision of capital was the most rapid and deliberate, the assumption of leadership in liberal commercial policy was halfhearted and faltering until the emergence of the European Common Market forced the country to a clear decision on the issue; and the assumption of responsibility as a key-currency country was not a deliberate decision but a recognition of a situation that evolved out of the dominating position of the United States as provider of capital and source of supplies during the period of dollar shortage. Unfortunately, the march of economic history was more rapid than the adaptive capacity of American economic policy could cope with, with the result that full acceptance of the responsibilities of world leader came only after the undermining of the United States dominant position had already got under way, and a sharing of responsibilities with the Common Market countries was required. In consequence, these responsibilities have proved a serious handicap to the intelligent formulation of domestic and foreign American economic policy, rather than a vindication of it.[3]

The consequences of the overvaluation of the dollar have been apparent in the economic problems of stagnation that have plagued the United States since 1957. The most fundamental consequence has been the combination of an abnormally high average level of unemployment with a chronic balance-of-payments problem, a combination that poses the classic policy conflict between the requirements of external and internal stability. Overvaluation means not only a

[3] For a detailed commentary on the changing position of the United States in the world economy, see my *Canada in a Changing World Economy* (Toronto: University of Toronto Press, 1962), chaps. i–v.

general tendency for domestic production to be uncompetitive with foreign production in the domestic and world markets, but the appearance of certain specific problems, notably a strong incentive for business to invest abroad rather than at home, thus strengthening foreign competition with transfers of capital and technical knowledge at the expense of domestic employment, and a reluctance on the part of recipients of military and development aid to spend their receipts on higher-cost domestic output. At the same time, the responsibilities the United States has assumed as center country of the world economy prevent the adoption of the most obvious — though not necessarily the most likely to be effective — methods of resolving the conflict. Consideration of the prestige of the currency, and the assumed moral obligation to foreign holders of it, together with the dangers of a speculative capital flight, preclude consideration of the only effective remedy consistent with the principles of economic liberalism, correction of the overvaluation by devaluation. Military and development aid commitments to other nations preclude a substantial cut in governmental transfers to other countries, which remedy might in any case be accompanied by a sufficient reduction in exports to render it nugatory. Commitment to leadership in the establishment of a liberal world economic system precludes resort to the protectionist remedy — a remedy which cannot be dismissed as economically disastrous when the alternative is a higher level of unemployment — or to restrictions on the flow of private foreign investment. With these methods of resolving the conflict between internal and external stability ruled out, all that is left to the policymakers are *ad hoc* devices for achieving the same effect as devaluation, restriction of capital movements, or protectionism, without incurring the associated opprobrium, or subtle policy combinations designed to avoid the conflict between external and internal stability by permitting an expansion of the economy without involving a worsening of the balance of payments. At the same time, a situation of abnormally high unemployment produced by an overvaluation of the currency whose relevance is either not appreciated or deliberately ignored offers boundless opportunities for irrelevant and frequently mischievous prescription based on erroneous diagnosis of the source of economic trouble.

To take the issues of erroneous diagnosis and prescription first, overvaluation of the currency inevitably focuses attention on the determinants of money costs of production on the one hand and of employability on the other. A universal complaint in countries with overvalued currencies is that money costs of production are too high because labor unions demand excessively high wages or businessmen demand excessively high profits, or because workers are less efficient than they ought to be or businessmen do not try hard enough to get out and sell. The choice of culprit depends on one's political philosophy, and no currency is truly overvalued unless fortified by a popular imagery of workers leaning on their shovels and businessmen resting on their backsides. The reflection of this type of analysis of the problem in government policy ranges from the devising of "guidelines" for wage and price determination, aimed at preventing wages and prices from becoming uncompetitive, to governmental intervention in wage and price determination and governmental measures to foster productivity and the adoption of more efficient techniques or production. On the side of the labor market, superficial diagnosis is exemplified by the attribution of unemployment to automation, and superficial prescription by the recommendation of a shortening of hours of work; a more subtle version of the same type of thinking, which has been influential in recent American policy with the right results for the wrong reasons, points to insufficient formal education or insufficient mobility as the source of unemployability. The summit of economic idiocy is only reached, however, with the contention that the unemployment statistics mismeasure the amount of "genuine" unemployment, and the recommendation that unemployment be redefined or unemployment insurance administration tightened up to reduce the measured amount of unemployment to a respectable level. The fallacy common to this whole category of analysis, it should be emphasized, is not that its proponents see a problem where none exists: in almost all cases there is a genuine problem, in the sense that the functioning of the economy falls short of an attainable ideal and could be improved by an appropriately devised policy. The fallacy lies in seizing on what may best be termed secondary structural defects in the functioning of the economy — myopic practices in wage and price determination, inadequate arrangements for retraining and relocation of the technologically unemployed, inadequate education of the labor force for flexibility in the face of change — and elevating each to a prime cause of general unemployment, in place of the real prime cause, deficient general demand.

As already mentioned, when direct resort to devaluation, restriction of capital outflows, or protectionism is ruled out, there is a strong tendency for policy-makers to resort to other devices for achieving the same results with much less efficiency; the makers of policy for the overvalued dollar have been no exception to this rule. In this context, United States policy-makers have been extremely adroit in confusing either themselves or the general public by exploiting both certain internationally accepted conventions and certain ingrained economic principles of American government that draw an artificial distinction between types of discriminatory intervention in international trade and payments that are consistent with a liberal international economic policy and types that are not. Thus, according to the conventions of liberal internationalism, dumping of exports is immoral; but subsidization of exports by provision of export credit on special terms is not only not immoral but a requirement of fair international competition. Similarly, the partial devaluation or discriminatory export subsidization — either interpretation is possible — implicit in the tying of foreign aid to domestic purchases is not "really" a violation of liberal international principles. Again, the contradiction between increased tariff protection and the pursuit of freer trade does not extend to the increased protectionism implicit in the government's efforts to divert defense expenditure to domestic sources; in this area, the government has in effect been enforcing a general tariff rate of 50 per cent, and in some cases tariff rates up to 100 per cent or more, in favor of domestic suppliers of articles of military use.[4] Yet again, restrictions on the free outflow of private capital are regarded as contrary to the principles of free enterprise; but the achievement of the same results by discriminatory subsidization of domestic investment through investment credits and liberalized depreciation provisions is not held to involve the same contradiction. Also in the area of capital flows, the use of governmental pressure and diplomacy to induce early repayment of intergovernmental debt is regarded as both legitimate and economically uncontroversial, whereas similar efforts to force repatriation of private foreign investment would be regarded as objectionable governmental interference.

[4] Cf. Statement of Charles J. Hitch, Assistant Secretary of Defense (Comptroller), *Hearings . . . , op. cit.*, pp. 49–58, esp. pp. 52–53. Since July 16, 1962, the Department of Defense has directed that goods and services for use overseas be procured in the United States whenever the cost of U.S. supplies or services (including transportation and handling costs) does not exceed the cost of foreign supplies or services by more than 50 per cent; the excess cost of procurement returned to U.S. sources under this directive in July–September, 1962, was 36 per cent. The military assistance offshore procurement program is subject to a 25 per cent differential and a further directive requiring military assistance funds to be spent in the United States so far as possible. Purchases for use in the United States are governed by the Buy-American Act and the Executive Order 10582, which establishes a margin of 6 per cent; but the discretion allowed to the Secretary of Defense has been used to direct domestic procurement at costs over 6 per cent above foreign costs. It is understood that increasing emphasis has been placed on domestic procurement since the testimony cited was given; the statement in the text reflects an informed estimate of the tariff equivalent of present procurement practice.

The examples cited refer to internationally accepted distinctions between legitimate and illegitimate forms of governmental intervention in international economic relations. A number of these distinctions, however, are accepted because the United States itself has insisted on them, and reflect a uniquely American dichotomy between the economic principles relevant to private enterprise and those relevant to government activity. The nature of the dichotomy is conveyed in Johnson's first principle of public finance in a free enterprise economy: Government must perform inefficiently whenever and to whatever extent the convenience of private enterprise requires. Consistent implementation of this principle, it should be noted, is essential to the survival of the free enterprise system, since it insures that private enterprise can always demonstrate its superior efficiency over government. Be that as it may, the exemption of the government's own economic behavior from the standards of efficiency normally applied, and the subordination of it to the requirements of balancing the balance of payments, have produced the paradoxical result that while the Administration has on the whole been moving toward a more liberal international economic policy as regards private trade, in its own domestic and international transactions it has been steadily elaborating the apparatus of protectionism, bilateral balancing, barter dealing, and exploitation of political bargaining power for economic ends that its policies for private enterprise profess to abhor.

The alternative line of policy-making open to a government faced with a conflict between external and internal stability owing to overvaluation of the currency is to attempt to apply policy combinations permitting expansion of the economy without threatening a worsening of the balance of payments. Since expansion of economic activity is certain to worsen the current account in the short run, whatever may be hoped for from faster growth and greater economic dynamism in the longer run, such policy combinations must seek to correct the weakening of the current account by a corresponding strengthening of the capital account. The macroeconomic thinking of Administration policy has been preoccupied successively with two general schemes for securing the desired result. The first was the much debated scheme for combining monetary expansion with open-market switches by the Federal Reserve from shorts to longs, the intention being to raise short yields relative to longs and so to prevent short-term capital outflows and gold losses while stimulating domestic investment. Whatever might have been expected of this policy — and empirical research on the term structure strongly suggested that the term structure was relatively insensitive to changes in the composition of the debt in public hands — it was not in fact pursued in any effective sense. As a result primarily of Treasury funding operations, the maturity of the debt in the hands of the public has in fact been lengthened appreciably, instead of shortened as the policy would require. Nor has the Federal Reserve been pursuing an expansionary monetary policy, if one measures policy by the rate of expansion of the active money supply, rather than by the two fallacious indicators of expansionism the Federal Reserve prefers to quote, the level of free reserves and the level of long-term rates relative to their level at the corresponding stage of the previous expansion. As has happened on previous occasions, the failure to pursue an expansionary monetary policy in any genuine sense has been interpreted to show that expansionary monetary policy has accomplished all that it is capable of, and that a resort to expansionary fiscal policy is now indicated. Hence the current recommendation of a tax cut, the hope being that domestic expansion will make domestic investment sufficiently attractive to domestic and foreign investors for its adverse effects on the current account to be offset by a matching improvement on private long-term capital account. This hope, it will be recognized, rests on an untested estimate of the relative responsiveness of the two parts of the balance of payments to economic expansion. While in principle some combination of fiscal expansion and monetary restriction is discoverable that will achieve internal expansion while preserving external balance, it is extremely doubtful that the Administration's economists have discovered it. It is perhaps for this reason that the Administration's proposals for tax reduction fall substantially short of what many experts believe would be necessary to achieve a satisfactory level of activity and employment. Nor, it might be added, is it at all clear a priori that expansion achieved by tax cuts directed mainly at personal income would contribute much to increasing the rate of economic growth.

Thus far I have been describing the conflict between internal and external balance that an overvalued currency necessarily entails, the obstacles to a solution imposed by the commitments the United States has assumed as center country in the international economy, and the types of makeshift policy to which the country is forced to resort when it seeks to raise its level of employment without correcting the fundamental source of its troubles by changing the value of its currency. In the course of the argument I have not had occasion to distinguish between the balance-of-payments problem and the gold reserve problem. For an international reserve-currency country like the United States has become, however, this distinction is vital. For a reserve-currency country can finance a balance-of-payments deficit for a substantial period without an appreciable loss of gold, and therefore without immediate pressure to correct for currency overvaluation, through the accumulation of its currency in the hands of foreigners. Conversely, the balance-of-payments situation of a reserve-currency country may be in fundamentally sound shape, and yet the country may be subjected to a dangerous and rapid depletion of its gold reserves through the encashment of its currency for gold by foreigners. Whether a reserve-currency country has a gold problem or not, therefore, depends on the behavior of the holders of its currency; and this depends on the confidence they have in it.

The key point in understanding the problems of a reserve-currency country, and one concerning which there is a frequent confusion, is that the holders whose confidence matters are not the generality of owners of liquid assets but the small group of central banks in the major financial centers. In the modern world all conversions of assets from one currency to another are exchanges with central banks; and an outflow of capital from the United States can only lead to a loss of gold if the central bank in the country to which the capital is flowing refuses to hold dollars but insists on receiving gold instead.[5] This is a potentially dangerous situation, since it means that the reserve-currency country must command the confidence of the fraternity of central bankers in its currency; it is a particularly dangerous situation for a country whose currency is overvalued, since the most potent disturber of confidence is a fear of devaluation. To allay that fear, the government and monetary authorities of an overvalued reserve-currency country must insist publicly and with conviction that the overvaluation will not be corrected — a ritual unfortunately only too well calculated to prevent any serious thought being given to the possibility until disaster strikes. They can also take steps to protect themselves against a run on their gold reserves by building up their facilities for borrowing back losses of reserves — as the United States monetary authorities have done by negotiating the special arrangements for the ten leading industrial nations to lend to the International Monetary Fund, by selling securities denominated in foreign currencies, and by arranging for currency swaps between the

[5] The United States may also lose gold if foreigners convert dollar balances directly into gold through the London gold market. (U.S. citizens are now prohibited from holding gold outside the United States.) This is the consequence of the stabilization of the London price of gold by a consortium of central banks in which the United States has a major participation.

Federal Reserve and foreign central banks — or by strengthening their capacity to forestall the development of runs — as by the consortium operations to control the price of gold in the London market, the freeing of interest rates on foreign deposits, and the development of Treasury and Federal Reserve operations in forward foreign exchange.[6] By these means, the defenses of the dollar against a gold run have been undoubtedly greatly strengthened in the past two years. But the means by which this strengthening has been accomplished, however gratifying the results may appear to the officials responsible — and especially to Mr. Roosa, who appears to have been the chief architect[7] — raise some ominous doubts about the ability of the Administration to overcome the stagnation of the economy, and particularly to take the necessary preliminary step of correcting the overvaluation of the dollar. In the first place, the arrangements have not included any sort of guaranty of the gold value of foreign holdings of dollars; without such a guaranty, the United States must be morally committed not to devalue. In the second place, the terms in which the new arrangements have been described and defended, especially by Mr. Roosa, convey a very strong impression of a solution to the world's monetary problems worked out by gentlemen's agreement among the small band of elect, according to a higher justice which the uninitiated can never hope to understand but must accept on trust. The failure of Montagu Norman and Benjamin Strong to solve the world's problems on the basis of informal co-operation among central bankers in the interwar period gives little basis for confidence in this approach. Moreover, reliance on it accentuates the dependence of the future of the dollar on the confidence of foreign governments and central banks — it is not for the sake of boast that the 1963 *Report of the Council of Economic Advisers* goes to such pains to emphasize that an expansionary fiscal policy has the advance approval of the Organization for Economic Co-operation and Development.

To summarize the main theme of this paper, the stagnation of the American economy during the past six years is attributable fundamentally to the overvaluation of the dollar. Unwillingness or political inability to face the fact of overvaluation, together with the commitments the United States has assumed as center country of the

---

[6] For a description of these developments see the papers by Robert V. Roosa and Charles A. Coombs, collected in Part 5 of *Factors Affecting the United States . . . , op. cit.*

[7] Cf. Statement of Hon. Robert V. Roosa, Under-Secretary of the Treasury for Monetary Affairs, *Hearings . . . , op. cit.*, pp. 116–21.

international economy, virtually condemns the Administration to adopt covertly protectionist policies in the economic affairs of the government, while preventing it from coping effectively with the problems of domestic economic stagnation. The conflict between external and internal stability could be resolved in two ways. The first, and more direct, method would be to correct the overvaluation of the dollar. One such solution would be a devaluation of the dollar — an increase in the dollar price of gold. To be consistent with the obligations of the United States as a reserve-currency country, an increase in the dollar price of gold would have to be accompanied by compensation to the holders of dollar balances. An alternative solution which I am prepared to recommend even though my study of the pronouncements of central bankers has convinced me of its laughable impracticability — if intrusted to management by central bankers — is the adoption of a floating exchange rate. The second, and less reliable, method would be an increase in international liquidity massive enough to induce an inflation in the rest of the world sufficient to bring price levels there back into conformity with contemporary exchange rates. Either method of resolution would entail a drastic departure from the present lines of United States economic policy — which probably means that the United States economy will have to sweat it out, under the weight of its cross of gold. The classical forces of competition in the world market will unquestionably correct the overvaluation of the dollar eventually, just as they eliminated the "chronic dollar shortage" of the postwar period. But the process will in all likelihood necessitate several more years of stagnation of the American economy,[8] and possibly involve a general recession in the non-Communist world economy as well.

[8] Houthakker (*op. cit.,* p. 298) argues that the pattern of overvaluation and undervaluation of currencies has not changed greatly in the postwar period, except as a result of exchange-rate changes. He discounts the quantitative significance for monetary adjustment of the recent rapid rise of German wages, which he maintains has largely been absorbed by increased productivity, and concludes that "even if the trends of the past two or three years continue, which is unlikely, it might take eight or ten years before the dollar ceases to be overvalued with respect to the mark."

Devaluation Is *Not* the Answer* ˋ

THE U.S. has for many years run a deficit in its international accounts, paying out more for imports, overseas military expenditures, foreign aid and foreign investments than it earns back from exports, overseas business profits and other sources. The result is an increase in foreign-owned dollars, which can be exchanged for U.S. gold.

However, devaluating the dollar, as Prof. Houthakker suggests, offers no miraculous cure for our balance of payments problem. A careful assessment of the nature of our present plight will show this quite clearly.

Houthakker stated that the U.S. dollar is overvalued in relation to all other major currencies except perhaps the Canadian dollar. He derives this conclusion from a comparison of living costs in various countries — an approach full of pitfalls.

For instance, according to the logic of this argument, if a package of goods costs less in Ireland than in Germany, it follows that the Irish pound is undervalued in relation to the mark. Similarly, if the same package of goods costs less in Japan than in Ireland, it means that the Irish pound is overvalued in relation to the Japanese yen.

The inadequacy of this approach is exemplified by the economic history of the postwar era. In the late 1940s and early 1950s the cost-of-living yardstick would have shown that the U.S. dollar was considerably more overvalued than at present. But, at the same time, there prevailed an acute world-wide dollar shortage. Describing the situation, Sir Geoffrey Crowther, Editor of *The Economist*, wrote: "It is difficult to believe that there can ever have been another case of a country where the demand of the rest of the world for its products was so urgent and its demand for the products of the rest of the world so indifferent."

Since then the cost of living has risen much more rapidly in Western Europe than in the U.S. According to the logic of Prof.

* From Robert Z. Aliber, "Devaluation Is *Not* the Answer," *Challenge*, December 1962, pp. 25–27. Reprinted by permission of *Challenge, The Magazine of Economic Affairs;* 475 Fifth Avenue, New York, New York 10017.

Houthakker's argument, this ought to have worsened the dollar shortage. But, instead, the dollar shortage has disappeared, and France, West Germany, and some of the other West European nations accumulated large dollar reserves. The cost-of-living yardstick is just too incomplete.

Seventeenth-century economists first advanced the theory that the national cost of living should determine exchange rates. Of course, relative price levels greatly influence exchange rates. But the rates are also partly determined by the flow of private capital, government expenditures abroad, foreign investment earnings, and so forth.

Even if international transactions were limited to imports and exports, the cost-of-living yardstick would be inadequate. The cost-of-living test could show prices somewhat higher in the United States than in other countries, but our commercial exports could still exceed our commercial imports. For example, in 1962 U.S. exports will approximate $21 billion while imports will run at about $16 billion. Perhaps $3 billion worth of U.S. exports will be government assisted — such as overseas shipments of surplus farm commodities and foreign aid. But *still* purely commercial exports will exceed imports in value by more than 10 per cent. The U.S. commercial trade surplus would be even larger if our country promoted exports as aggressively as, for instance, West Germany and Japan.

Fundamentally, the large U.S. commercial trade surplus results from two factors. First, a great many products such as refrigerators, coal, phonograph records, construction machinery, poultry and corn are produced more cheaply in the U.S. than abroad. Second, the U.S. holds a technological lead in the design of such items as large jet aircraft and complex computers. The competitiveness of U.S. prices for many products, and design superiority in others, made it possible for exports to exceed imports from Western Europe by 45 per cent in 1961.

Most supporters of dollar devaluation would probably agree that the free exchange market provides a far better test of the value of a nation's currency than the cost-of-living comparisons made by statisticians. In their view, the dollar is overvalued because in almost every year since 1949 the U.S. has run a balance of payments deficit. But it does not automatically follow that just because a nation has a payments deficit its currency is overvalued, nor conversely that a balance of payments surplus proves that a currency is undervalued.

That deficit countries have overvalued currencies and surplus countries have undervalued currencies is not an analytical proposition but, rather, a definitional one.

A nation's balance of payments surplus may stem from a great many factors. Switzerland, for instance, has run up large balance of payments surpluses, partly because of the inflow of money from Latin America, the United States, Britain and West Germany. However, at the same time, Switzerland has run large deficits in all its basic accounts except short-term capital flow. France's balance of payments surplus dates from 1958, when Gen. de Gaulle returned to power and instituted tight monetary policies. The coincidence with De Gaulle's return to power is so striking that one can only wonder what will happen when the Fifth Republic gets a new leader.

There are not many countries which actually have undervalued currencies. For a time during the 1950s it appeared that the West German mark and the Italian lira were *somewhat* undervalued, but this is no longer the case. In March, 1961 the Adenauer government upvalued the mark by five per cent, which may have been partly responsible for the switch from a surplus to a deficit in the West German balance of payments. Presumably, the upvaluation ought to have exerted a downward pressure on domestic prices by encouraging imports and discouraging exports. However, prices have increased sharply in Germany and it appears they will continue to do so. For example, since the spring of last year the West German cost of living has risen by six per cent while industrial wages have increased by about 15 per cent.

Similarly, the value of the Italian lira has been whittled down by recent developments. Slowly, Italy's surplus manpower is being absorbed by the rapidly expanding industries of Northern Italy, West Germany, France and Switzerland. At the same time, the equalization of the wages received by women and the reduction of the workweek suggests that both wages and prices will continue to rise while Italy's payments surplus may be further reduced. For example, since early 1961 Italy's wholesale prices have risen by 2.9 per cent while hourly factory wages have risen by about 10 per cent. During the first seven months of 1962 Italy had a total balance of payments surplus of only $2.4 million, compared to a surplus of $577 million in 1961.

Full employment, or even overfull employment, prevails in Western Europe and this enhances the pressure for higher wages and a shorter workweek. Over the coming years West European prices will probably continue to rise more rapidly than U.S. prices. At the same time, the rate of U.S. investment in Europe is likely to slow down. Consequently, the price and cost factors which in the last several years have led to the large U.S. payments deficit will diminish and the U.S. competitive position relative to Europe should become more favorable.

The excessive 1949 devaluation of leading West European currencies in relation to the dollar gave the European a cost advantage in many areas, but they were unable to take full advantage of the circumstances because of their limited production capabilities. In recent years, as West European output increased and exports expanded, they relaxed many of their restrictions on the import of U.S. goods. This facilitated the expansion of U.S. exports to Western Europe and helped maintain a satisfactory U.S. payments balance. By 1959 the West Europeans had removed most of their quantitative restrictions on the import of American goods which had been adopted for balance of payments reasons. So, this means of keeping payments in balance was no longer available.

This is why the large U.S. payments deficit occurred at about the same time that most European currencies were freed from extensive exchange controls. Since then a more rapid rise in European prices and costs has tended to assist the necessary international adjustment. At the same time, the large balance of payments deficit has forced the U.S. to initiate overdue remedial measures. The payments deficit focused attention on the need for a more adequate export credit program, more generous depreciation allowances and tax reforms. It has also convinced the U.S. government to exert pressure, especially on West Germany, Italy and the Netherlands, to extend aid to underdeveloped countries and to force greater scrutiny of U.S. military expenditures abroad.

U.S. defense expenditures abroad in recent years have amounted to about $3 billion annually. These sums have exceeded the deficit in U.S. payments. In the early postwar years U.S. expenditures abroad were welcomed as a means of relieving the pressing dollar shortages of most European nations; indeed, the size of the expenditure was partially tailored to the size of their dollar shortage. Even though the dollar shortage has disappeared, it has been difficult to alter the size of these expenditures. If in the future our North Atlantic Treaty Organization allies assume a larger share of the common defense program, the "overvalued" dollar might become an "undervalued" dollar.

If the U.S. were to devaluate its currency in terms of gold, almost every other industrial nation would undoubtedly do likewise by a similar amount. Many British economists, in fact, feel that the pound sterling would have to be devalued to an even greater extent. This points out one of the paradoxes of the current international payments structure. It is that there can be deficit countries with "overvalued" currencies without there being surplus countries with "undervalued" currencies, for the sum of payments deficits greatly exceeds the sum of the payments surpluses. For example, in 1961 aggregate worldwide deficits in basic accounts exceeded surplus by more than $1.2 billion (the previous year the disparity was $1.5 billion). This imbalance would have been much greater if short-term capital movements were included. In its 1962 annual report, the International Monetary Fund, in a masterful understatement, noted that: "The excess of deficits thus implies that the country figures tend to err more frequently in the direction of overstating deficits or understating surpluses."

WALTER S. SALANT AND ASSOCIATES

Policy Recommendations for the International Monetary Mechanisms*

THE NEED TO IMPROVE THE INTERNATIONAL
MONETARY MECHANISM

THE PRESENT international monetary system is essentially a system of quasi-fixed exchange rates with international reserves held in gold and national currencies (principally dollars and sterling). The price of gold in terms of dollars is fixed, and other currencies are pegged to the dollar, thereby providing a fixed structure of exchange rates among various currencies. The pegs are adjustable, however. Adjustments have been made with sufficient frequency in the postwar period to keep the possibilities of further changes alive in the minds of central banks and private owners of capital.

In our view, fixity of exchange rates is a virtue. Fixed rates remove much of the uncertainty which would otherwise be inherent in international movements of goods, services, and capital. They tend

* From Walter S. Salant et al., *The United States Balance of Payments* (Washington, D.C., 1963), pp. 245–51, 255–62. Reprinted by permission of The Brookings Institution.

to increase the volume of trade and productive international investment, thus contributing to efficient use of world resources and to economic welfare. The more certain it is that the rates will be maintained, the greater are these advantages. If confidence in the maintenance of exchange rates becomes firmly established, it is likely that the process of adjusting balances between countries will begin to resemble more closely adjustment among different regions of a single country, in which equilibrating movements of capital induced by small differences in interest rates play a major role. Such a development, although involving some loss of national autonomy in monetary policy, would ease the adjustment process. In addition, by increasing the economic interdependence of the Free World countries, it may tend to increase their political cohesion. We believe, therefore, that the present system of fixed exchange rates should be strengthened so as to preserve and enhance its advantages and mitigate its disadvantages.

The main disadvantage of the fixed rate system as it now exists is that it requires countries whose payments are not in balance to restore balance more rapidly than may be consistent with important domestic and international objectives. The speed at which a payments imbalance can be eliminated without endangering such objectives depends on its cause. One class of imbalances results from excesses or deficiencies of demand induced by inflation or deflation in individual countries. Although imbalances of this class call for prompt adjustment, they no longer occur frequently in the advanced industrial countries. Contracyclical policies are reasonably effective in preventing deflation; the internal objective of price stability is, in most of these countries, an effective restraint on inflation caused by excess demand.

The other class — and the most frequent cause of serious imbalances in these countries — is structural change. Under liberal trading conditions and freedom of international capital movements, and with increasing similarity in the patterns of demand and output in the large countries, structural changes must be expected to cause larger imbalances than they formerly did. Moreover, in an increasingly dynamic world, the pace of structural change must be expected to increase. Under these conditions, it will be quite unwarranted to assume that large deficits necessarily call for drastic action designed to restore payments equilibrium quickly. Imbalances caused by structural changes call for structural adjustments — shifts in the use of capital and labor with a view to changing the pattern of production, expansion or modernization of the capital stock in particular industries, or other measures which require several years to be effective. They require time, not drastic action aimed at achieving an immediate result.

The great danger of a system of fixed exchange rates operated with the existing and foreseeable level of reserves is that it does not permit deficits to be financed long enough to make the kind of adjustments that are most often needed. Deflationary measures, the classical means of improving the balance of payments, cut employment and real incomes — effects which are neither politically feasible nor economically desirable in a modern industrial country. In the United States, large absolute reductions in real income cause only small decreases in imports, and these decreases are partly offset by decreases in exports, so that very substantial declines in total production and income are necessary to induce relatively small improvements in the net balance of payments. Furthermore, higher interest rates, while discouraging domestic investment, may not be effective in attracting capital to a weak currency when strong currencies are available.

Measures to reduce imports by raising tariffs or imposing other trade restrictions are equally undesirable for reasons which hardly need to be re-emphasized. So are direct controls on capital movements and cuts in foreign aid and government spending abroad for defense and other purposes. Nor is it desirable for advanced creditor countries which are having balance-of-payments difficulties to transfer to primary producing countries their burden of payments adjustment by curtailing lending to those countries.

The combination of the normal fixity of exchange rates with the possibility that they will be changed when an imbalance has persisted long enough to be judged fundamental makes rapid adjustment especially difficult. The possibility that a weak currency will be devalued discourages equilibrating capital movements and fosters disequilibrating movements, and does so at all times, not merely in times of crisis. By doing so, it reinforces the basic factors originally responsible for the currency's weakness. Disequilibrating capital movements cannot be counteracted by small differences in interest rates, because such differences have no effect when there is no confidence that the parity will be maintained. Moreover, when the authorities decide to devalue — either because they wish to or because they can no longer withstand the pressure on the currency — they are usually eager to convince the market that the new exchange rate can be held. One way to accomplish this purpose is to make the devaluation so great that no one will doubt that the new rate can be maintained. As a result, currencies which have been overvalued before their parities or altered are likely to be undervalued afterward. Thus, the adjustable peg system has these disadvantages: the efforts to defend an exchange rate are complicated by speculation; devaluations are likely to be too long delayed; and devaluations are likely to be excessive when they are finally made.

If an international payments system is to provide the benefits of fixed parities without these disadvantages, it must generate confidence in the fixity of the parities. Given greater liquidity, confidence in the fixity of parities would probably develop, because it would gradually be recognized that enough time was available to restore equilibrium in the payments of the major countries without revaluation of their currencies.

The belief that balance-of-payments adjustments at fixed parities are possible if enough time is available rests on several considerations. First, some imbalances are caused by random or cyclical developments which are likely to average out over sufficiently long periods, even in the absence of corrective governmental policies.

Second, some imbalances result from shifts in the competitive position of major national industries, resulting in losses of exports or increases in imports. These competitive challenges often induce competitive responses, although these responses may take several years to affect the balance of payments. The response of the U.S. automobile industry to the challenge of foreign cars is an example.

Third, these competitive responses can be supplemented by government policies to stimulate investment in export and import-competing industries and thus to improve a country's competitive position. Substantial increases of investment in such industries, whether induced by competition or by government policy, often take several years to be effective. In fact, if they are not offset by reductions in other forms of expenditure on goods and services, they may temporarily increase deficits and require several years to be effective in reducing them.

Fourth, the international transactions of governments are now a large component of total international transactions. Given a reasonable degree of international cooperation, without which any system is in danger of breaking down, it should be possible to adjust some of these transactions gradually in ways that reduce imbalances.

Fifth, although money wage rates can be reduced in industrial countries only at the cost of increased unemployment and slower growth, a country with a deficit can reduce the general level of money costs per unit of output slowly over time by preventing the general level of its money wage rates from increasing as fast as output per man-hour. If these reductions in money costs are not completely off-set by increases in profits, a country can improve its competitive position, provided that prices in competitor countries do not fall as rapidly. This proviso suggests the desirability of international cooperation regarding cost and price policies.

Sixth, after the fixity of exchange rates is assured, countries that can pursue flexible fiscal policies can correct imbalances without reducing domestic output or inflating the domestic price level. They can do so by changing interest rates relative to those abroad and offsetting the domestic effect of changes by fiscal policy.

It is to be noted, however, that nearly all these forms of adjustment require time to be effective. In a world in which internal adjustments cannot be made quickly without sacrificing objectives more important than balance in international payments, a system of fixed exchange rates can work only if long periods are allowed for the adjustments to take place.

THE CHARACTERISTICS OF A SATISFACTORY INTERNATIONAL MONETARY MECHANISM

An international monetary system which enables countries to restore balance-of-payments equilibrium slowly over periods of several years must have the following characteristics:

1. *It must provide enough liquidity at the outset to finance substantial imbalances while adjustments are taking place, and it must provide for increases in liquidity as the need for liquidity grows.* Liquidity need not take the form entirely of reserves owned by the countries to whom it is available. It can be provided wholly or partly in the form of drawing rights, support extended to deficit countries by surplus countries, or other credit facilities extended either directly or through international institutions. In any case, because imbalances arising both from persistent and stubborn shifts in basic transactions and short-term capital movements are potentially quite large and are likely to grow, the increases in international reserves and other forms of liquidity must be substantial.

2. *Additional liquidity which takes the form of credit should be available readily and promptly, and for a period long enough to permit elimination of the deficit.* Substantial amounts should be obtainable automatically by deficit countries. By agreement, additional amounts should be made available to countries with particularly intractable balance-of-payments problems if appropriate mea-

sures for dealing with these problems are being taken. Preferably, the amounts available automatically should take the form of open-account facilities with ceilings, within which there should be no fixed repayment dates. The discretionary amounts should be repayable on terms that reflect a realistic assessment of the time required to bring the balance of payments into adjustment.

3. *The possibility of shifting reserves from weak to strong currencies must be prevented.* If additional reserves were held in national currencies, this possibility would be a continuing source of instability and would impose constraints on the countries whose currencies were used as reserves. Avoiding these constraints would require an agreement under which countries with strong currencies would support weak currencies by maintaining or, if necesary, increasing their holdings of the weak currencies. Such an agreement would have to be accompanied by guaranties of the values of the reserve currencies. Even then, any deficit country that avoided reserve losses by incurring increased liquid liabilities to others would be likely to regard the increases in these liabilities in the same way that it now regards reserve losses. It would thus feel the very constraints which an improved system should seek to eliminate. These problems would be avoided if industrial countries committed themselves to hold a substantial fraction of their reserves in an international institution, with creditor countries accumulating credits denominated in an international unit of account and debtor countries accumulating similarly denominated debits or reducing previously acquired credits.

4. *For such a system — or indeed for any system — to work, it is probably necessary that the principal financial and industrial countries consult fully and frequently and coordinate policies that have substantial effects on international payments.* This consultation and coordination is likely to be particularly necessary in view of the magnitude of imbalances that are likely to develop. It should include wage and price and commercial policies as well as monetary and fiscal policies.

The main objection often made to providing additional liquidity, especially if it is available unconditionally, is that countries may use the resulting leeway to indulge in inflationary excesses without fear of running into payments difficulties. This danger cannot be completely discounted. Nevertheless, the advanced industrial countries have increasingly recognized the dislocations caused by rising prices and have developed a disposition to curb inflationary developments on purely domestic grounds. The additional discipline provided by the balance of payments is indiscriminate in its application; it induces restraint without regard to whether internal conditions call for restraint or expansion. While it adds something to the disposition of advanced countries to curb internal inflation, its benefits in such situations are far less than the social costs it imposes when domestic expansion is needed.

A second objection to the provision of additional liquidity is that it would permit countries to continue misallocation of resources and deprive them of the stimulus to improve productivity. To the extent that deficits result from the loss of export markets, however, the decline of profits resulting from their loss gives business firms ample incentive to develop new products and to increase efficiency, whether or not more liquidity is provided. In fact, countries that seek to eliminate deficits quickly without incurring the social costs of otherwise undesired monetary and fiscal restriction usually resort to import restrictions, exchange controls, and similar devices. Such measures worsen, rather than improve, the allocation of resources and reduce incentives to increase productivity. Deflationary measures also restrict investment and hamper modernization and innovation. Indeed, since efforts to improve resource allocation and increase efficiency usually require several years to be effective, and are more likely to be made in an atmosphere of general expansion and unrestricted foreign competition, they are remedies that argue in favor of, rather than against, the provision of additional liquidity.

We do not suggest that the developing countries be included in any arrangements for additional reserves or automatic access to credit facilities. Their balance-of-payments problems are very real and pressing, but they are of a long-term character and cannot be solved by mere increases in liquidity. In these countries, import demand chronically outruns ability to import, either for monetary and fiscal or for structural reasons. Thus, the key problem is the amount of aid which the advanced countries should provide to finance imports of goods and services by these countries, since the financing they provide will be used to purchase imports rather than to accumulate reserves.

If an adequate system of international liquidity is developed, it should be possible to dispense with changes in exchange parities, and to replace the adjustable peg system with permanently fixed parities. It will take a number of years, of course, to demonstrate the effectiveness of the system and to build up confidence in the permanence of the parities.

When that confidence has been established, a further useful step would be a widening of the limits around the par values within which the actual market rates are allowed to fluctuate. The limited fluctuations of exchange rates permitted by such a widening of the support points would have a number of advantages. First, they would give rise to capital movements which, under the conditions specified, would be stabilizing rather than destabilizing and would reduce the need for using official reserves and credit facilities. Second, they would permit greater variability in short-term interest rates among countries than would be possible with absolutely fixed market exchange rates, thus permitting somewhat greater national autonomy in monetary policies. Finally, even the limited variation in exchange rates possible with support points of 2 per cent to 3 per cent on either side of parity would be helpful in promoting balance-of-payments adjustment. Among industrial countries producing similar products, price elasticities in international trade over periods of several years can be expected to be high, so that small changes in exchange rates would have considerable influence on trade balances.

AN ALTERNATIVE INTERNATIONAL MONETARY MECHANISM

If it becomes clear that agreement on a satisfactory liquidity mechanism cannot be obtained, the United States must seek an alternative.

We have already stated why a one-step devaluation of the dollar is not desirable as a means of dealing with the balance-of-payments deficit. Also it is not a desirable way of improving the international monetary mechanism. While such a devaluation, if accompanied by corresponding devaluations of other currencies, would result in a one-step increase in the money value of the world's gold stock, it might add little to total world liquidity, even in the short run. Some gold might be released from private hoards as holders took steps to realize their capital gains. But, on balance, it seems likely that devaluation would make individuals and central banks more reluctant than they are now to hold liquid assets in the form of dollars and other national currencies and more inclined to hold gold. In any case, although devaluation would probably give some stimulus to gold production, this would not provide continuing growth in liquidity commensurate with world needs. Moreover, the benefits of devaluation would be distributed unequally and capriciously among countries. In sum, devaluation might seriously impair the operation of the existing monetary mechanism and would not put anything better in its place.

We also reject the alternative of using comprehensive controls over imports of goods and services and over capital movements in order to maintain a fixed exchange rate, although this does not exclude the possibility of informal restraints on U.S. purchases of new issues of Western European securities. The substantial economic and political costs involved in such a reversal of postwar policy would exceed any gains it could yield.

The best alternative to a system of fixed rates with provision for increasing liquidity, in our view, would be a modified system of flexible exchange rates consisting of a dollar-sterling bloc and an EEC bloc. There would be relatively fixed rates within each bloc and flexible rates between them. Adoption of this system would imply cutting the tie between gold and the dollar.

In contrast to a fixed-rate system, a system of flexible rates has the advantage that both the short-run competitive position can be changed and the longer-run structural adjustments can be made without general deflation of money costs in deficit countries and general inflation in surplus countries. A reduction in the value of a deficit country's currency reduces the prices of its exportable goods in foreign currencies, thereby encouraging foreign demand for them and raising their prices in its own currency. The rise in the domestic price reduces the domestic market for them, releasing more of existing supplies for export. It also raises the prices of imported goods in the national currency, discouraging their importation and shifting domestic demand toward domestically produced goods and services. Thus the competitive position of the deficit country can be improved rapidly without deflation. The reverse changes occur in surplus countries without inflation.

The changes in demand and prices which occur under flexible rates also facilitate the necessary longer-run structural adjustments. In a deficit country, resources are attracted to production of exportable goods and import-competing goods because their prices rise more than those of domestic goods. Under fixed rates this incentive to shift resources occurs only through deflation of the general price level, with smaller downward pressure on the absolute prices of internationally traded and import-competing goods and services than on other goods and services. A flexible rate program avoids the adverse effects that downward pressure on prices has on output in all sectors. So long as the country whose currency declines in value maintains fiscal and monetary policies that prevent prices from rising as much as its exchange rate falls, it can make the necessary structural adjustments without the destructive consequences of general deflation.

Since there appears to be little need to adjust the exchange rate between the dollar and the pound, it should be possible for the United Kingdom and the United States to agree on arrangements for mutual currency support. With such arrangements, the present rate between their currencies could be maintained indefinitely, the present restrictions on the outflow of British and sterling area capital could be removed, and the British and U.S. capital markets could be integrated. Such cooperation would be in the interests of both countries. Countries whose economies are closely aligned to the United States and the United Kingdom — those in the Western Hemisphere and Scandinavia, most of those in Asia and the Middle East, and some in Africa — would probably want to peg their currencies to the dollar-pound.

Within Western Europe, the logic of economic integration demands that fixed parities be maintained among the members of the European Economic Community a fixity which they could easily effectuate. Countries whose economies are closely aligned to the EEC — such as Austria, Greece, Switzerland, North Africa, and the French Community — would presumably wish to tie their currencies to those of the EEC, which could be done through cooperation of the appropriate monetary authorities. The only significant fluctuations, therefore, would be in the rates between the dollar-sterling bloc on the one hand and the Western European bloc on the other. Violent changes in these exchange rates would be prevented by intervention of the stabilization authorities in the foreign exchange markets. In practice, we would expect the range of these fluctuations to be limited.

There are many advantages to recommend this modified flexible exchange rate system. Primarily, it would allow the United States to pursue most of its national objectives without undesirable balance-of-payments constraints. The United States would enjoy greater national autonomy in the use of fiscal policy, since the external consequences of such policies would be offset by movements in the exchange rate. The fluctuations in themselves would provide a mechanism through which basic imbalance between currency blocs could be corrected.

Such a flexible exchange rate system would also reduce the need for international reserves. A deficit country would no longer need substantial reserves to relieve pressures on its exchange rate. Support for its currency would automatically be provided by the surplus countries of its own bloc. If a whole bloc were in deficit, the surplus countries of the other bloc would be induced to enter the market in support of the weak currencies to prevent unwanted appreciation of their own currencies. Although this system could be adversely affected by destabilizing speculation, such speculation would probably be smaller than under the present system of adjustable pegs with inadequate liquidity. With flexible rates, speculation would involve the risk of substantial loss as well as the prospect of substantial gain. Moreover, the central banks of the major countries, acting in cooperation, could easily counter the pressure of destabilizing speculation. Cooperation would be forthcoming because both appreciating and depreciating countries have an interest in preventing the exchange rate from reflecting destabilizing speculative forces.

One objection sometimes made to a flexible exchange rate for the dollar is that the maintenance of the present gold parity and the present exchange rate between the dollar and other currencies are essential to U.S. national power or prestige. We think this view mistaken. The power and prestige of the United States derive in large degree from its economic strength and vigor, which in turn depend on its high productive potential and its success in using that potential. Failure to maintain the present gold parity would do far less to damage U.S. prestige than continued failure of the economy to operate at or near capacity. One of the most striking lessons of international currency experience since the First World War is that countries which have sacrificed basic national objectives in order to maintain overvalued parities have suffered major economic losses and in the end have failed to maintain the rate. If the United States sacrificed needed domestic production in an effort to maintain the dollar exchange rate in the face of continuing balance-of-payments deficits and inadequate provision for international liquidity, it would lose power and prestige, as well as the output that it could otherwise have produced.

Nevertheless, there are some true costs in adopting our second-best, two-bloc proposal. The volume of international trade and capital movements between the members of the two blocs would probably be smaller than under a system of fixed parities with adequate provision for international liquidity. While the costs to traders of fluctuation in exchange rates would be tolerable as long as there was an active forward exchange market, the discouraging effects might still be substantial. Some unity and cohesion of the Free World might therefore be sacrificed. That is why we regard the two-bloc system as inferior to a system of fixed parities with adequate provision for liquidity. We believe its cost to be less, however, than that of any alternative that would be available if the improved fixed parity system could not be attained. The two-bloc system would eliminate the deflationary bias inherent in fixed rates with inadequate liquidity. It would contribute to fuller use of productive capacity and more rapid economic growth so that, despite the impediment of rate flexibility, world trade might be larger than under the present system.

The Balance of Payments:
A Political and Administrative View[*]

MY WORKING view of the balance of payments, a reasonably commonplace one, places it on three levels. At the bottom and most basic for policy is the net balance of goods and services. This yielded a surplus of $3.8 billions in 1960, $5.4 billions in 1961 and $4.8 billions in 1962, the result of a merchandise surplus of roughly the same size and a (net) investment income which had reached $3.3 billions in 1962. Against this were military expenses (amounting to $3.1 billions in 1962), net travel outlays (amounting to about a billion in 1962) and a variety of other payments and remittances including United States Government grants of nearly $2 billions. Preliminary figures for 1963 show an improvement in the net balance of about a billion dollars, the result of further increases in investment income, a modestly larger increase in exports than in imports and a slight decline in military spending.[1]

At the next level are the long-term private capital outflows ($2.8 billions net in 1962) and government loans (amounting net to $1.5 billions in 1962). This outflow creates a corresponding claim by Americans on overseas resources and portends a possible later improvement in the payments balance as the result of interest, dividends and repatriated earnings. These items were evidently about the same in total in 1963 as 1962. But this was as the result of a sharp curtail-

---

[*] Reprinted by permission of the publishers from John Kenneth Galbraith, "The Balance of Payments," *Review of Economics and Statistics*, May 1964 (Cambridge, Mass.: Harvard University Press), Copyright, 1964, by the President and Fellows of Harvard College.

[1] In the last three years, apart from secondary discussions and memoranda, I have been concerned with the balance of payments problem on two major occasions. In 1961, during the first weeks of the new administration, I had general coordinating responsibility for the special message which was transmitted to the Congress in February 1961. On my return from India in the summer of 1963, I was asked by President Kennedy to review the problem and report. This paper draws on this experience. But, as will be evident from the context, it does not reflect accepted policy and cannot be read as any indication thereof. Moreover it was, in some measure, my task in 1963 to consider ultimately rather than presently necessary action.

ment of private capital outflow in the second half of the year following a very large increase in the first half. Long-term outflows are continuing at a low level as this is written in early 1964.

In 1962 all the foregoing transactions — the so-called basic balance — involved a deficit of $2.1 billions. There has been a deficit in this account in every year since 1947. At its highest in 1959 it amounted to $4.7 billions.[2] In late 1963 and early 1964, the movement in this deficit was sharply down.

The third level is ultimately derivative from the foregoing. Dollar claims accumulate as the result of the foregoing commercial transactions and capital movements. They can be held in the form of dollar deposits or converted into foreign currencies or gold. In the main they have been held in dollars and thus the large accumulation of current dollar claims in recent years — from around $7 billions in 1950 to some $25 billions at present. But some $7 billions has been converted to gold and removed from the monetary gold stock in the last six years. This has been the most visible and publicized aspect of the balance of payments problem and also the one that is most purely a consequence, rather than a cause, of changes at the other levels.

Few public problems can ever have been so ingeniously contrived to maximize difficulty as that of the balance of payments. There has continued to be a question as to whether there is a problem. There has been a puzzling choice between real and spurious solutions. And each of the real solutions has been protected by a stout framework of vested ideological and economic interest reinforced, in some cases, by distinctly non-secular conviction. The sources of difficulty may be dealt with under the following heads:

(1) The question as to whether there is a problem;
(2) The tendency to technical escape;
(3) The temptation to cosmetic or public relations action;
(4) The vested resistances to action.

Each of these barriers requires a word. I will then turn to the progression of measures appropriate for handling the balance of payments problem in various forseeable situations.

II

The conviction that there can be no real problem is partly subjective, a delayed accommodation to a change in the American position that

[2] Data from *Statistical Supplement to Survey of Current Business* (1963), and *Survey of Current Business* (June 1963), as used in *The United States Balance of Payments in 1968*, The Brookings Institution (Washington, D.C., 1963). Appendix Tables for 1963 from *Economic Report of the President.*

is difficult mentally to embrace. For decades the American net balance on goods and services account was insouciantly strong. Almost everyone came to regard this as the normal situation. The internal economy is effective for its domestic function; if this is so and given the history can there by any *real* poverty in means of external payment? There can be, of course. The United Kingdom and the Soviet Union are contemporary examples of countries with an effective internal economy which have to tailor policies to available external resources. Many others have had to do so in the past. High employment or favorable living standards do not signify any particular availability of external resources. Nonetheless favorable domestic performance is assumed to accord the United States some kind of exempt status.

A less subjective view, leading also to the conclusion that there is no problem, stresses, in effect, the inevitability of corrective development. This no longer depends on the compensating mechanism of classical international trade theory. Instead there is a surrogate belief that sooner or later countries that are in surplus will follow policies or encounter misfortunes that will dissipate it. Such a belief is evidently back of the Brookings Institution[3] forecasts of the balance of payments in 1968. After much good analytical work, some of it supporting a different result,[4] the authors agree that prices and wages in the European Economic Community countries will rise sufficiently in relation to those of the United States so that our competitive position will be restored and our balance on merchandise and service account will become sufficient for our needs. This could happen. Circumstances are currently favoring the Brookings forecasts. Costs and prices have been rising in the Common Market countries; as this is written a number are heavily in deficit and the EEC as a whole is running a small deficit. Continuing adversity in agricultural supplies would add to these tendencies. But this is only one possibility. Renewed pressure by American unions, coupled with the effects of the tax cut and the pull of demand could lead to renewed pressure on our prices. At the same time the Common Market countries, which are sensitive to inflation, could exercise stronger control of wages and costs. The conclusion that the payments deficit will be eliminated by favorable price and cost movements is not a prediction but a hypothesis. Other hypotheses are plausible. And one cannot accept the most agreeable hypothesis as the basis for

[3] *Ibid.*

[4] The Brookings authors take a pessimistic, and I think realistic, view of the effect of Common Market commercial policy on American imports. (See below.)

policy. As Edward M. Bernstein has observed, there would be risk in assuming that "other countries will (solve the problem) for us by their inflation."[5]

However the conviction that nothing is seriously wrong is not at its most influential in isolation. It is most important in conjunction with the belief that certain technical steps will correct matters in comparatively painless fashion. These measures are thought now to be excluded by traditional attitudes, psychological resistance or the absence of technical sophistication and comprehension. These steps allow for what I have called technical escape.

III

The two principal avenues for technical escape are, first, devaluation to either fixed or floating exchange rates and, second, proposals for increasing international liquidity either by informal arrangements for the holding of more short-term dollar assets by foreign central banks or by formal revision of the charter of the International Monetary Fund or some evolution thereof. Both owe something to the tendency to decide questions without reference to their political or administrative context or, less forgivably, to admit in principle of these considerations and then proceed to firm recommendations as though they did not exist. There is also a not unimportant tendency to confuse nicety of point or originality of position with practical feasibility.

There is no question that devaluation, either to a new fixed parity with other currencies or to a floating rate, can for many countries be a highly serviceable remedy for balance of payments disequilibrium. It is a step which, because of political or psychological resistances, is usually postponed well beyond the time when it should be taken. At any given time there are usually a number of countries which are resisting such action and for which it would be sound policy.

Here is part of the problem. In seeking generality this action is discussed as though policy that is applicable (past or present) to Turkey, Canada, India or Chile were equally applicable to the United States — that what relatively small countries may do vis-a-vis

[5] *The Brookings Report on the Balance of Payments in 1968*. An Analysis prepared for the Joint Economic Committee (Sept. 23, 1963), published in *The United States Balance of Payments*, statements by economists, bankers, and others, Joint Economic Committee, U.S. Congress, 88th Cong., 1st sess. (1963), 60–72.

a very large one is equally possible for a very large one vis-a-vis all the smaller ones.[6] I agree with Secretary Robert Roosa that the position and employment of the dollar as a reserve currency excludes devaluation to fixed parities as an equilibrating policy and even more specifically rules out recourse to fluctuating rates.[7] Certainly anyone advocating such a policy must show that its applicability to a reserve currency such as the dollar is as great as (say) to the *Lire* or *Real*. But a more compelling question is whether and why other countries should accept such action on our part. Canada can devalue vis-a-vis the United States; but why should she or any other country dissipate present trading strength and accept a competitive disadvantage when, by simple parallel action, she can restore the previous parity. With flexible rates one could imagine a period of intense jockeying (and therewith the forced holding of dollars of which much point has been made) and additionally perhaps some outbreak of competitive devaluation. But it is hard to imagine other competitive countries according the United States a durable advantage.[8, 9]

But most of all there are the practical questions. As the United States is governed, no move to alter parities could be taken without advance rumor and discussion. This would be the signal for massive and massively publicized withdrawal for the very large short-term balances. (One wonders if some balances do not remain here because of the virtual certainty of notice under our system of taking delicate decisions after due public discussion). This would then seem to force the action. The aspect of political weakness and even helplessness in such a development is obvious. No administration with any regard for its political reputation would invite it. Those who speak of devaluation either to fixed or floating rates *as serious policy* must show

[6] See for example the discussion by Harry G. Johnson and Richard E. Caves in *Papers and Proceedings,* American Economic Association (May 1963), pp. 112 *et. seq.*

[7] ". . . the United States dollar — firmly tied to the price of gold — plays a key role in the world payments system, supplementing gold as a source and store of liquidity and as a trading currency." Address before American Economic Association and American Finance Association (December 28, 1963). mimeographed.

[8] The experience of 1933 cannot be cited in this connection for United States action in the spring of that year was an adjustment to the earlier devaluation by other trading nations led (or confirmed) by that of the United Kingdom in 1931.

[9] Everyone who participates in this discussion has a Swiss banker whom he can quote. Mine, responding some years ago to the question of whether the Swiss would devalue in response to such American action said: "It might be late the same afternoon."

how these manifestations of political disarray and weakness could be avoided.

As a practical matter, the United States must correct disequilibrium when it arises within the framework of fixed parities. Devaluation to fixed or floating rates is a course of action vouchsafed only to lesser and differently governed powers.

The improvement of liquidity arrangements, which has also been the lodestone for much economic discussion, does not, of course, alter the underlying situation. It merely extends the time during which the disequilibrium may be corrected and it minimizes the danger of politically or economically disturbing movements of short-term funds in the interim. Those who regard it as a remedy are, in effect, saying that the disequilibrium is self-correcting in the long run. And this, to repeat, is a hypothesis and not an assured development on which policy can be based.

This does not at all invalidate the case for measures to increase international liquidity. It means only that such action is not remedial. Moreover the strength of our position in negotiating such arrangements, like many other aspects of our foreign policy position, is related to the balance of payments. We are in an excellent position to take leadership in this effort when our balance of payments is strong and other countries are worried. We are in a poor position to assume leadership if our balance of payments is weak and our negotiators appear as supplicants. If our payments balance should remain reasonably strong in the next months this would be the best possible reason for pressing ahead on improved liquidity arrangements.

IV

Public relations and cosmetic measures assign a curative role to quantitatively insignificant measures; to those that are unimportant within the relevant time span; to those that alter the appearance but not substance of the problem. While export sales promotion, the stimulation of tourist travel in the United States, placing limits on duty-free tourist purchases abroad,[10] and campaigns to sell savings bonds to soldiers, may be justified by marginal calculations of effort and accomplishment, they cannot alter the fundamental position. Nor will debt prepayments which have had the purely cosmetic effect of dressing up the current balance at the expense of later ones. The self-congratulation accorded these measures in the past has had

[10] A measure with which I was associated.

important elements of self-delusion which has excused the postpone-
ment of more effective measures. However it was also based partly
on the belief that the disequilibrium was transitory. The important
thing, therefore, was to quiet public fears, if necessary by stimulated
action, in the interim. It will be evident in this respect that cosmetic
measures are not without possibility of damage.

A more defensible example of cosmetic action has been the sale
of securities denominated in foreign currencies and the manipulation
of short-term interest rates to encourage holding of dollar balances by
foreigners. Neither deals with the factors making for a growth in
short-term claims; both seek to stabilize these holdings and thus keep
them from affecting the more publicized phenomenon which is the
gold outflow. As with liquidity arrangements they have interim value
if longer-term corrections are at work. But also, as with the liquidity
discussion and other cosmetic action, they can also be devices for
evading or concealing the need for more fundamental and more
disagreeable action.

This is especially true of interest rate policy for it is united with
the interests of a strong and exceedingly subtle lobby. The rate of
interest in the United States can only be understood as the one price
that has been, in some sense, consecrated. Producers of wheat, copper,
cotton and even steel are assumed to prefer higher prices for the
larger revenues they return. Those who lend money, in contrast, are
permitted to urge higher interest rates not for the greater return but
as a selfless step designed to protect the nation from the evils of soft
money, loose financial practice and deficient economic morality. An
economist who sees the need for a higher weekly wage may well be
suspected of yielding to the unions; one who urges an increase in
the rediscount rate is, however, invariably a statesman. This should
not keep anyone from penetrating to the fact. There is a lively,
insistent and durable preference by the money-lending community
for high rates of return; this is related to an intelligent view of pecu-
niary self-interest. It would be astonishing were it otherwise — were
this community or its spokesmen in the unique position of resolving
these issues in accordance with an essentially socialist criterion.

In recent years persistent unemployment and the concern of a
liberal administration for improved economic behavior made lower
interest rates a natural object of policy. The balance of payments has
become the most telling argument against lower rates. A cosmetic
measure has thus acquired the support of very influential individuals
and institutions interested in higher rates for their own sake. Those
who have urged higher interest rates for balance of payments reasons

have often and perhaps most frequently been interested in something else. Moves to raise interest rates have thus achieved a dangerously exaggerated reputation as a balance of payments remedy. They continue to have such a reputation. Meanwhile any action here leaves the underlying disequilibrium untouched.

V

From the foregoing it will be clear that one does not propose fundamental action on the balance of payments problem until he reaches the basic levels of the problem and in their consequential magnitudes — the question of long-term capital flows and, even more basically, that of domestic costs and prices, commercial policy and the overseas operations of the United States government. At this point one encounters the resistances to action.

Until the summer of 1963 the Treasury, the department of the government with primary responsibility for the problem, was reluctant — perhaps understandably for it was not a decision to be taken lightly — to give the payments problem priority over the maintenance of a free capital market. The State Department continues to consider the balance of payments problem subordinate to trade and tariff policies and perhaps even large issues of European unification. It is also subordinate to a given troop commitment in Europe. Elsewhere, and less seriously, the payments problem encounters the fear of extending commercial relations with the Communist countries and reluctance to impose additional restrictions on the use of aid funds. Assuming all are fully effective these resistances amount to a total ban on all remedial action. Such vested bureaucratic interest cannot, obviously, be the basis for policy. The question is what is the appropriate progression of policy measures when action is required.

VI

The first and most obvious step for a country faced with a balance of payments problem is to control access to its capital markets. This precaution is exercised by all countries at the present time whether their payments position is strong or weak with the possible exception of West Germany. The condition for capital exports is, evidently, a surplus of external resources; if these are unavailable then capital exports should obviously be curtailed.

The United States Treasury, it seems certain, now shares this conclusion. There remains the question of whether it yet has an effective instrument of control. The Interest Equalization Tax requested with the retroactive effect on July 18, 1963, was a hurried response to the large capital outflows then taking place. It does not touch direct investments of American corporations which are still large and which until 1963 accounted for decidedly the larger part of the private capital outflow. (In 1962, $1.6 as against $1.2 billions.) The tax is unpredictable in its effect. While pending, it has acted as a near-ban on the issues to which it applies. Rejection, or even final passage with the removal of uncertainty (and given the superior efficiency of the American issues market), could bring a flood of new issues. A more effective procedure would be to establish a capital issues committee, authority for which exists under section 5(b) of the Trading with the Enemy Act of 1917. Subject to appropriate exemptions it would control access to the issues market. Under the same authority, it would also authorize expansion and take over investment by American corporations involving substantial commitment of dollars abroad. These are not pleasant measures. However they are the ones coordinate with the task. Past practice has been to deny the need for such measures, sometimes with some firmness and then, as in the case of the Interest Equalization Tax, to resort to them *in extremis*. The wiser course would be to admit of the possible need and be prepared to act if and when the measures are required.

However the control of capital outflows, though immediately indispensable, is not the ultimate solution. The ultimate corrective for balance of payments disequilibrium is at a more basic level. It is a surplus in trade and service account sufficient to cover necessary military and other obligations abroad and to allow for long-term capital outflows as an equilibrating item. These, in turn, add long-term support to the payments position.

Military obligations must always be examined in the full context of other policy. We cannot do abroad what we do not have the external resources to pay for; the price of present military outlays could always be a more severe contraction later on.

For the near future saving on military outlays means redeployment of forces. The Department of Defense in recent years has made considerable effort at overseas economy; it is doubtful, in consequence, if further restrictions on travel by dependents or troop outlays would produce savings consonant with the loss in morale. (It is to be recalled that civilians are free to spend and reside abroad as they wish.) However no given force can be considered sacrosanct. A strong balance of payments is a factor of major importance in national position and leadership. In the past our force commitment to France and Germany has poured dollars into these countries and, by weakening our balance of payments, weakened our bargaining position vis-a-vis these countries. The military commitment has then been defended on the grounds that it is necessary to our position in Europe. The flaws in this logic suggest the need for a catholic view of the issue. Deployment must also be examined in light of modern technical developments in air transport and long-range fighter aircraft. These now give the option of deploying troops so as to minimize foreign exchange cost without lessening their real as distinct from symbolic effectiveness.

VII

In past times the first step of a country faced with balance of payments difficulties was to discourage imports, either by tariffs or quotas. This is now highly unfashionable — and it is too bad. Tariffs — the general or selective discouragement of imports by increasing their prices — are, in many respects, the simplest and most straightforward of measures for dealing with disequilibrium. They place most reliance on the price system; they less immediately involve questions of national security than cuts in military outlays; it is more nearly consistent with the liberal tradition to regulate the movement of goods than that of (say) people.

However tariff action is now excluded as a policy by a general commitment to lower tariffs, by the fear of retaliation by other countries and, perhaps, by the underlying fear that any step toward protection as a matter of national policy will unduly encourage latent protectionist attitudes in the United States. These positions are not above challenge. One may wonder if tariff reduction is an absolute good to be placed above national interest; many who fear retaliation on tariffs disregard it where exchange depreciation is concerned. But the immediate question is whether we are to have an essentially passive policy toward increased protectionism elsewhere. Although American protectionists are still considered uniquely omnipotent, it is doubtful, in fact, if they approach the influence or self-confidence of European agriculturists and industrialists.

In fact a reconsideration of present trade policy is of prime importance — and remains urgent despite the recent improvement in the payments balance. We have a substantial surplus on merchandise account — in 1963 an estimated $4.5 billions. But in light of our other overseas commitments we need a large balance and this one could be considered, in fact, perilously small. Last year it was between estimated receipts of $25.8 billions and estimated payments of $21.4 billions. A comparatively small change in exports or imports can thus be a source of great gains or grave losses.

There are a number of minor but useful steps that need to be taken on trade policy. Trade with the Communist countries has suffered from exaggerated, erroneous or unexamined views of the efficacy of economic warfare and the fear of officials of being called soft on Communism. (Concern is not to maximize the public interest but to minimize the outcry from the domestic Right.) Countries receiving aid could, perhaps, be more effectively impressed with the importance of employing their free dollars in the United States. . . .

VIII

At the most fundamental level, the balance of payments also requires restraint on prices and wages — an effective management of the cost-push. The recent improvement in the payments balance also leaves this of undiminished importance. It would be more urgent and presumably more difficult as we add the effects of a tax cut to general expansion. That some rely on European inflation as a remedy is sufficient reason to minimize our own.

More generally it will be clear, an effective balance of payments policy requires an open mind toward a large number of measures which we have come to consider settled and in some degree sacred — uninhibited capital exports, progressive tariff reductions, given troop commitments. The common reaction to remedial action involving these matters tends to verge on outrage — "Look what that man is suggesting now." Unfortunately where the payments balance policy is concerned there are no convenient measures. If there were they would be put quickly and painlessly into effect when trouble threatens. It is the British postwar experience that the problem yields rather quickly once there is determination to act. But developing the public determination that is necessary to reverse the normal and comfortable course of policy can take a long while. Our experience has not been different.

The Interest Equalization Tax[*]

A YEAR AGO, our balance of payments was deteriorating sharply. That deterioration was due almost entirely to accelerating capital outflows, and particularly to an unprecedented outflow of portfolio capital. The rate at which new issues of foreign securities were being purchased had more than tripled in the previous 18 months, and the volume during the first six months of 1963 reached a total of $1 billion.

As a result, the deficit in our international accounts — apart from all special inter-Governmental transactions — jumped from the already high 1962 level of $3.6 billion to an annual rate of $5.3 billion in the second quarter of 1963. If allowed to continue, that deficit would have undermined the international stability of the dollar.

Today our balance of payments situation is much improved, and the dollar is strong. Judging from data at hand, the deficit for the fiscal year ending tomorrow, calculated on the same basis, will be well under half that of the preceding fiscal year.

Paralleling this improvement, confidence has been restored in our ability to achieve a balance in our payments within a reasonable time. This, in turn, has staunched the drain on our gold stock. After declining by an average of $1.7 billion a year over the 1958–60 period, and by roughly half that rate during 1961 and 1962, our total gold stock today is virtually unchanged from ten months ago — by far the longest period of stability during the past six years.

However, we must not succumb to any illusion that the progress of the past year means the end of our long-standing balance of payments problem or allows us in any way to relax our drive toward equilibrium. The hard fact is that after six consecutive years of large deficits — adding up to a total of $21½ billion on the basis of regular transactions — we face once again this year the unhappy task of financing a sizable, even though substantially reduced, imbalance in our payments.

Roughly half of our payments improvement for the past twelve

[*] Statement before the Senate Finance Committee, June 29, 1964.

months can be traced directly to diminished outflows of capital into foreign securities. But the basic problems giving rise to the enormous capital outflow in 1962 and early 1963 have not yet been solved. Were we not now to proceed with enactment of the proposed Interest Equalization Tax, demands from abroad for portfolio capital would once again quickly converge on our market in a volume far larger than we could sustain. We simply cannot afford to pay the price such an event would exact in terms of dangers for the dollar and losses of gold and confidence — thus undercutting our whole international financial position.

THE NEED FOR THE TAX

The need for the Interest Equalization Tax has arisen out of a combination of circumstances here and abroad that led to a rapid acceleration in foreign demands on our capital market. In the short space of the first six months of 1963, purchases of new foreign issues — the overwhelming bulk from other industrialized countries — reached a seasonally adjusted annual rate of $1.9 billion. That was $800 million higher than the already swollen 1962 total and three and one-half times the 1961 level. In addition, the indications were that potential borrowers in Europe and Japan, who had already increased their demands on our market dramatically, were scheduling still larger borrowings in this country.

This surging flow of foreign borrowings simply swamped the real progress in other areas of our balance of payments. As a result, our overall deficit on regular transactions rose to an annual rate of $5 billion during the first half of 1963, sharply above the totals of $3.1 and $3.6 billion in 1961 and 1962, respectively. These increases, as shown by tables 1 and 2, paralleled the swelling outflow of portfolio capital into new foreign securities.

This rise in the outflow of portfolio capital reflected neither financing of U. S. exports nor the more general balance of payments needs of the borrowing countries. On the contrary, more and more of the new flotations in our market were designed to finance local projects of businesses or governments in countries already enjoying relatively strong or improving external positions. Many of the new borrowers did not require foreign exchange, but only desired greater amounts of fresh capital to support their own internal growth. Because their own capital markets were both narrow and costly, those borrowers desiring funds were naturally attracted by our relatively low long-term interest rates and by the ease with which large amounts of funds could be obtained in our well-developed market. As a result, a large portion of the outflow of portfolio capital, by providing more dollars to those who simply wished to exchange those dollars for their own currencies, was adding roughly equivalent amounts to our deficit. The dollars in turn were flowing into central banks and becoming a claim on our gold.

Appraising the same facts from a European vantage point, the most recent Annual Report of the Bank for International Settlements reached the same conclusion. That Report, which is representative of responsible and official European opinion, noted, in speaking of 1963, that ". . . instead of being a net exporter of capital, which would seem the appropriate structural position, Europe was a large net importer of capital — which in the main has been flowing into reserves."

Purchases of foreign portfolio securities by Americans do in time lead to a return flow of interest and dividend income. But this potential return is spread over many future years, while the entire outflow of principal is immediate. For instance, during both 1962 and 1963, years when the outflow of U. S. portfolio capital into foreign securities averaged about $1¼ billion, the increase in our income from such securities amounted to only about $50 million a year. Clearly, calculations of earnings possibilities many years in the future cannot, in the situation we face, substitute for the urgent need to protect the dollar by bringing the current portfolio capital outflow within the limits of our immediate capacity to lend.

THE NATURE OF THE INTEREST EQUALIZATION TAX

In the light of these circumstances, prompt and effective action to reduce the outflow of portfolio capital was essential. The proposal before this Committee is designed to achieve that result by means of an excise tax levied on the American acquiring directly from a non-resident foreigner a foreign stock or debt issue maturing in more than three years. While the tax is payable by the American purchaser, the impact will be effectively passed on to the foreign issuer in reduced prices for his securities.

The rate of tax is graduated so that its net effect is to increase by about one percent the annual cost of capital to a foreigner raising money in our market, thus bringing this cost to a level more comparable to the costs he would face abroad. The result for foreigners would thus be similar to an increase of one percent in our entire structure of long-term interest rates.

Finding our market more costly, many potential foreign borrowers will seek the funds they require at home, or in other foreign markets, instead of aggravating the strains on our own position. Similarly, American investors will find the net yield on American securities relatively more favorable than yields provided on outstanding foreign securities purchased from foreigners, and will tend correspondingly to reduce their purchases of such securities.

We view the proposed tax purely as a transitional measure. As our own payments come into equilibrium, as the expansion in our own economy reduces incentives to export our capital, and as the capital markets of other advanced countries develop the capability of more adequately meeting their internal needs, this special tax can and should be removed. H. R. 8000 contains a termination date of December 31, 1965, to assure that it will not be prolonged beyond the time of need. At the same time, because of the urgency of dealing with the problem, President Kennedy proposed that this tax become generally effective July 19, 1963, the day following its announcement in his Special Message on the Balance of Payments. Any other course would simply have been an open invitation for potential borrowers and lenders to accelerate their plans and crowd into our market before the effective date of the tax. Our balance of payments most certainly could not have borne such a strain.

On the other hand, making that proposed effective date known to the market has permitted careful Congressional consideration of this important piece of legislation without the atmosphere of haste and urgency which would inevitably have developed in the face of accelerating capital ouflows. The House, in approving this proposed date, recognized that any other course would only have rewarded those few who have been willing to gamble on the possibility that a late effective date would be enacted, at the expense of the great majority who have already adjusted their transactions in the light of the proposed July 1963 effective date.

Transactions in foreign securities between residents of the U. S. would not be subject to tax, and Americans would, of course, be able to sell foreign securities free of tax to foreigners in markets both here and abroad. Thus, active trading markets in the more than $12 billion of foreign securities already held by Americans will be maintained, and these securities will fully maintain their value. The passage of time since last summer has clearly proved that the provisions of the tax regarding outstanding securities are workable, and that they contribute substantially towards improving our payments position.

The proposed bill would exempt a variety of acquisitions from foreigners where this is possible without undermining the effectiveness of the tax and where imposition of the tax would work at cross purposes with other objectives. The exclusion from the tax of obligations maturing within three years assures that the great bulk of our export financing and normal recurring international business will not be impeded. Further to assure unimpeded export financing, longer-term export paper is specifically exempted, as are bank loans made in the ordinary course of business.

Other important exemptions would be provided for the governments and businesses of less developed countries and for direct investment. In addition, the President would be provided discretionary authority to exempt in whole or in part new issues from a particular country in those instances in which he determines that application of the tax would imperil, or threaten to imperil, the stability of the international financial system. This exemption is designed as a kind of safety valve for use only when it can be clearly established that, as a direct consequence of the tax, a foreign country would be forced to take such drastic measures that international financial stability would be imperiled. Any such showing would be dependent upon a highly unusual set of circumstances, and in my opinion the necessary conditions are today met only by Canada. . . .

BALANCE OF PAYMENTS IMPACT

The effectiveness of the proposed tax in reducing the outflow of portfolio capital — and the key importance of this in terms of the entire balance of payments — is clearly revealed by the results since last July. After running at a rate of $5 billion during the six months prior to the President's Message in July 1963, the deficit on regular transactions dropped sharply to a rate of $1.6 billion during the second half of 1963 and to $700 million during the first quarter of 1964. The first quarter results reflect a number of special factors which had the effect of substantially but temporarily reducing the deficit. Among these was an unusual and temporary short-term capital inflow during March that was fully reversed early in April, thus adding to the deficit being incurred during the current quarter.

A number of factors, including a sizable rise in exports, have contributed to the improvement in our balance of payments since last July. However, the single, largest element in this improvement is the sharp decline in net purchases of foreign securities. Comparing the nine months before the tax was proposed with the nine months since that time for which full data are available, the outflow into foreign securities dropped from $1,985 million to $290 million at seasonally adjusted annual rates, a reduction of $1.7 billion in the annual rate of outflow. . . .

We have, of course, also been closely following trends in bank lending, in view of the possibility that foreign borrowers might seek to shift to that kind of financing. While analysis of detailed information supplied by the banks on their commitments for the first five months of 1964 does not suggest any significant direct substitution for market financing, the total volume of short- and long-term loans outstanding rose sharply in 1963 and during the first quarter of 1964. The rise started early in the spring of 1963 and became particularly noticeable during the fourth quarter.

A good part of this increase is clearly related to the surge in American exports over the same period. But, in addition, it is possible that, in adjusting to the tax, borrowers in a few countries under balance of payments pressure — notably Japan — have made greater use of bank loans. While some initial reactions of this kind are not surprising, and there are now some indications of a leveling off of the loan volume, future trends will clearly require continuing surveillance. We will promptly recommend to the Congress appropriate changes in the bank loan exemption should it appear that such loans are in fact being utilized to any significant degree as substitutes for market financing.

THE TAX AND OUR OVERALL BALANCE OF PAYMENTS PROGRAM

This tax is only part — although a crucial part — of a comprehensive balance of payments program. A satisfactory long-run solution for our payments problem depends on a more vigorous and efficient domestic economy, capable of sustained productive expansion with stable costs and prices. Major steps to support this objective were taken in 1962 with the investment tax credit and the liberalization of depreciation allowances. They were followed this year by the $11.5 billion reduction in individual and corporate tax rates.

Together with responsible wage bargaining and pricing policies, these fiscal measures are now strengthening our basic competitive position at home and abroad, and our basic trade outlook is favorable. Greater prosperity at home, with greater profitability of investment here relative to the returns available from foreign investment, will reduce the incentive for direct investment abroad and encourage the retention of funds at home where their investment in domestic projects will create more jobs for Americans.

We have also placed great emphasis upon reducing the net flow of dollars abroad as a result of Government programs. For example, between 1960 and mid-1963, our annual rate of net military expenditure abroad was reduced by more than $500 million. That portion of our economic assistance provided by AID in the form of U. S. goods and services rather than dollars has been raised from less than one-third in 1960 to over 80 percent for current commitments.

President Kennedy last July scheduled an additional reduction of $1 billion in the annual rate of overseas Government expenditures by the end of this year. President Johnson is determined to achieve that target.

As you can see, visible gains are being made towards solving our basic payments problem. But we must not permit them to be drained away in a renewed outflow of portfolio capital.

ALTERNATIVES TO THE TAX

While appreciating the need to restrain the outflow of portfolio capital, some have suggested that there are preferable alternatives to the tax. One would be an attempt to drive up our entire structure of long-term interest rates by about 1 percent. Such a drastic tightening of credit, if possible at all, would clearly work against all that we are trying to achieve to reduce excessive unemployment and encourage the investment that creates jobs and promotes efficiency. The Interest Equalization Tax increases the cost of our money to foreigners, just as would a sharp increase in our own rates. But it will do so without the disrupting effects on the entire domestic economy of an attempt to artificially force our long-term rates to unrealistically high levels. . . .

CONCLUSION

The Administration has proposed this temporary tax with reluctance, but the need for action to restrain the outflow of portfolio capital is clear. The workability and effectiveness of our approach have been demonstrated. It is far preferable to any alternative that has been suggested.

Our international competitive position is strengthening, and other measures to achieve lasting improvement in our payments are bearing fruit. But these measures take time, and meanwhile our deficit remains sizable. Failure to enact this tax would stimulate a resurgence of capital outflows with dire effects on our balance of payments. . . .

The Marginal Cost of Hot Money*

THE FEDERAL RESERVE SYSTEM in July, 1963, raised the discount rate in order to ease the balance-of-payments position of the United States by attracting short-term capital. Adverse effects on the level of domestic activity were to be avoided by isolating the long rate from the impact of higher short rates. The purposes of this note are (1) to point out that, apart from any effects on domestic activity, this policy has an important cost which has been neglected in current discussion and (2) to estimate this cost. The cost is found in the increased flow of interest payments needed to service the greater volume of foreign-held liabilities.[1] Since the intent of the policy is to attract capital, any estimation of the cost must measure it as a marginal rate of return paid on the induced liabilities.[2]

An increase in the short-term rate of interest should both encourage foreign short-term funds to flow into the country and discourage domestically owned funds from being placed abroad. As the international deficit of the United States is currently computed, an inflow of short-term foreign funds will not affect the recorded deficit but will ease pressure on official holdings of international liquid assets; a reduction in the outflow of domestically owned funds will reduce the recorded deficit. However, the two results are similar in their cost aspects in that an inflow of foreign funds will involve the payment of interest to foreigners and the retention of domestic funds will eliminate a potential receipt of interest from foreign sources.[3]

The capital movements which ensue from a change in relative

---

* Reprinted from "The Marginal Cost of Hot Money," by H. Peter Gray, in *The Journal of Political Economy*, April 1964, pp. 189–92, by permission of the University of Chicago Press. Copyright 1964 by the University of Chicago.

[1] See *Committee on the Working of the Monetary System — Report*, Cmnd. 827 (London: Her Majesty's Stationery Office, 1959), paragraph 438, for an example of British recognition of this cost.

[2] This cost also exists when short-term rates rise as a result of a domestic boom. In such a case the international cost is a necessary concomitant of domestic prosperity. The return on the cost is the moderation of the boom and the consequent impediment to domestic price increases.

[3] No further differentiation will be made between these two effects.

international short rates are adjustments of stocks to a new array of rates of return. The impact of the new policy, therefore, can be expected to be felt quite quickly. On the other hand, the increased flow of interest payments is continuous until the policy is reversed.

If a commercial bank were to increase the rate of interest it paid on time deposits to counteract a deposit drain, the policy would enhance the liquidity of the bank's balance sheet at the expense of its profit-and-loss statement.[4] Similarly, an increase in the discount rate would improve the liquidity of the United States international balance sheet to the detriment of its balance on current account and international net worth. The increased flow of interest payments would comprise both the return paid to the newly attracted capital and the additional payments made on outstanding foreign-held liabilities as they realized the new, higher yields. However, the full effect of the new yields on outstanding liabilities would not be felt immediately since the new rates of return would become applicable only as the existing securities matured and the funds were reinvested.

TABLE I — SHORT-TERM LIABILITIES TO FOREIGNERS REPORTED BY BANKS
IN THE UNITED STATES

[Millions of dollars]	
Deposits:	
Demand	$6,875
Time	4,278
U. S. Treasury bills and certificates	9,091*
Other	2,039

* Excludes $2,976 million non-interest-bearing U.S. notes held by the I.M.F.

Source: Preliminary data for May 31, 1963, from *Federal Reserve Bulletin,* July 1963, p. 1020.

The marginal cost of induced international capital movements will depend upon the volume of funds attracted, the new short rate, the volume of liabilities held prior to the rate change, the difference between the old and new average rates of return per annum paid on previously held funds and the time needed for the new average rate to be achieved.

[4] See David A. and Charlotte P. Alhadeff, "A Note on Bank Earnings and Saving Deposit Rate Policy," *Journal of Finance,* XIV (September 1959), 403–10.

Let C = increase in interest payments per annum made to foreigners (in dollars).

I = volume of induced capital movements (in dollars).

F = volume of short-term liabilities held prior to the rate increase (in dollars).

r = average rate of return paid on newly attracted funds (in per cent per annum).

d = difference between the old and the new average rate of return paid to the short-term liabilities held before the rate increase (in per cent per annum).

The marginal cost of the induced capital funds is the total increase in interest payments divided by the volume of the induced capital movements. If we assume d to achieve its full value instantaneously,

$$\frac{C}{I} = \frac{Ir + Fd}{I} = r + \frac{F}{I}d.$$

This formula can be used to estimate the annual cost to the United States of the interest-induced capital movements.[5]

Estimates of the United States short-term liabilities to foreigners reported by banks amounted to $22,283 million in May, 1963.[6] A subdivision by category is given in Table 1.

It does not seem unreasonable to assume that the rate of return on time deposits will increase by 0.25 per cent.[7] The rate paid on bills and certificates and other liabilities may be assumed to increase by the same amount (0.5 per cent) as the increase in the discount rate. On the basis of these assumptions, the increase in interest payments made on liabilities held prior to the increase in the discount rate, Fd, will amount to $66 million.

The volume of induced capital movements may be assumed to earn a rate of return equal to the new discount rate of 3.5 per cent. Secretary Dillon has estimated the size of induced capital movements to be approximately $1 billion, of which $500 million will be increased short-term liabilities to the United States and the other $500 million

[5] This estimate of the marginal cost will exaggerate the cost for the first year while securities mature. After one year, the formula will be accurate. The exaggeration will probably be very small after ninety-day bills mature.

[6] Excludes liabilities payable in foreign currencies. ($129 million).

[7] There is room for such an increase without change in Regulation Q. The majority of time deposits of official foreign institutions are earning 3½ per cent (see Caroline H. Cagle, "Interest Rates on Time Deposits, Mid-February, 1963," *Federal Reserve Bulletin* [June 1963], p. 772).

will comprise decreased foreign placements of United States capital.[8] Thus the marginal cost of the funds is

$$\frac{C}{I} = \frac{(0.035)(1,000) + 66}{1,000} = 10.1 \text{ per cent.}$$

The increase in the United States short rate will attract short-term capital to this country at an estimated marginal cost of approximately 10 per cent. This estimate involves certain assumptions, and these can now be examined individually to see whether they are likely to have biased the result.

1. International short-term capital movements are influenced by interest rate differentials so that, for the change in the United States short rate to exert its full force, foreign interest rates must not change. In fact the Euro-dollar rate increased very shortly after the announcement of the increase in the discount rate, with the result that the estimates of capital movements by Secretary Dillon are likely to have been overly optimistic. Any exaggeration of the volume of capital movements induced by the change in the discount rate will have imparted a downward bias to the estimate of marginal cost. If the total induced inflow amounts to only $500 million, the marginal cost is 16.7 per cent and if only $250 million, 29.9 per cent.

2. Liabilities of foreigners to non-banks were not included in the volume of short-term liabilities outstanding prior to the rate increase, F, because of the inadequacy of the data.[9] Consequently, the estimated increase in the interest cost of previously held funds will be in error on the low side.

3. The rate of return on newly acquired funds and the increase in the rate of return on previously held funds may have been overestimated. However, if the volume of capital movements induced by changes in United States short rates (changes in the differentials if all foreign rates stay constant) is a linear function of these changes, the failure of the short rates to change *pari passu* with the change in the discount rate will have led to an overestimation of the volume of induced capital movements. Thus, if d and r have been overesti-

[8] This estimate has been derived from Dillon's statement of July 8 in Joint Economic Committee, Congress of the United States, *Hearings on The United States Balance of Payments* (88th Cong., 1st sess., July 8 and 9, 1963), p. 26. Dillon's statement relies heavily on studies by Peter B. Kenen and Benjamin J. Cohen, *op. cit.*, pp. 153–208.

[9] These liabilities are estimated at $642 million as of December 31, 1962 (see *Federal Reserve Bulletin*, June 1963, p. 870).

mated, *I* will have been overestimated by the same proportion and the estimate of the marginal cost will be unaffected, although the absolute increase in interest payments will have been reduced.

4. The possibility of the redistribution of foreign assets as a result of the increase in the short rates has not been taken into account. Any movement of foreign-owned assets out of lower- into higher-yielding assets will increase both the marginal and the absolute cost of the induced capital movements. While balances of official institutions are not sensitive to changes in international differentials,[10] they are sensitive to changes in relatve rates of return among different types of assets.[11]

5. If the whole yield curve moves upward despite official effort to maintain the long rate at its original level, the increased rate of return on these funds, when the securities have matured, will augment the cost of attracting short-term liabilities by an increase in the discount rate.

A policy of inducing a net inflow of short-term capital by means of an increase in the short rate has, therefore, a balance-of-payments cost. The lack of attention paid to this aspect of the interest rate policy may be due to the fact that the major concern is with the overall supply and demand for United States dollars — the cash flow — rather than with any secondary effects of the achievement of the necessary increase in international liquidity.

But manipulation of short rates has another disadvantage in addition to its international cost; the results of such a policy can easily be reversed before the deficit has been eliminated. An increase in foreign interest rates will either result in the exodus of the attracted capital or will require an equal increase in the United States short rate. If foreign rates increase, the capital outflow will add to the deficit and to the pressure on the gold stock; if United States short rates are raised to preserve the existing differential, the international cost will increase and the likelihood of preventing repercussions on the level of domestic activity reduced. The desirability of the policy depends upon the value given to the avoidance of overt interference with international transactions, the length of time for which it permits such interference to be avoided together with the probability of its being avoided completely, and the cost of the policy in terms of the reduction of international net worth. The cost is not independent of the other two considerations, since a reduction in net worth

[10] Cohen, *op. cit.*, p. 206.
[11] Cagle, *op. cit.*, p. 772.

increases the probability that additional measures to defend the dollar will have to be undertaken.

Alternative methods of meeting the current balance-of-payments deficit without contravening the ground rules of liberal international-ism also have their costs.[12] Permitting gold reserves to be reduced saps public confidence; tying of loans and aid reduces the value of funds to the recipient nations, and discrimination in favor of domestic industry in defense expenditures results in "invisible" tariffs of over 50 per cent in some cases.[13]

A policy of manipulation of short-term rates to attract short-term liabilities buys time. In the absence of other measures designed to correct the basic problem and/or autonomous trends toward fairly immediate removal of the deficit, time is likely to be expensively purchased. At a marginal cost of 10 per cent repatriation of the increased earnings will have nullified the liquidity gain in ten years, leaving only the liability.

[12] For example, devaluation, dumping, restriction of capital movements, and protectionism (see Harry G. Johnson, "An Overview of Price Levels, Employ-ment, and the Balance of Payments," *Journal of Business*, XXXVI [July 1963], 285).

[13] See the statement of Charles J. Hitch, Assistant Secretary of Defense (Comptroller) in Sub-committee on International Exchange and Payments of the Joint Economic Committee, United States Congress, *Hearings on the Out-look for the United States Balance of Payments* (87th Cong., 2d sess., December 12, 13, and 14, 1962), p. 52. See also Johnson, *op. cit.*, p. 285.

CONCLUSION

The dollar deficit has been the product of many forces operating simultaneously. On these forces have been imposed a series of policy measures designed to reduce the size of, and even to eliminate, the deficit. The autonomous forces and the countervailing measures are so numerous, varied and interrelated that it is virtually impossible to measure the magnitude of the effect of any single influence.

To some extent the emergence of a "significant" deficit in 1958 was due to the recovery of Western European production to a competitive position in the world economy and all of the readjustments which the recovery entailed. Foremost among these were competition in markets previously considered safe for United States firms, like Latin America, and the outpouring of capital to Europe. If the resurgence of Europe was the prime cause of the end of the so-called dollar shortage, the net result was not one of decreasing United States international net worth. The dollar deficit was, with the exception of one or two years, always a problem of lessening liquidity when the surplus on current account exceeded those transactions on capital account which did not generate foreign assets (e.g., foreign aid, soft-currency loans, etc.), and the United States was not "saving" sufficiently quickly. The net accumulation of assets in Europe has been a sign of strength, not weakness, for the dollar in the long run.

To reduce strain on the dollar's liquidity the Federal Government instituted many measures. Some of these measures were designed with an eye to political expediency and practicality rather than to any inherent desirability or effectiveness of the measure. Indeed, as proposal after proposal reached the Congress, there was an inevitable aura of *ad hoc* actions. Yet, despite the crucial failure to stimulate sufficiently an economy operating at an unsatisfactorily low level (and this failure was more a question of domestic economics than of concern with the deficit), the Federal Government has pursued an enlightened course of restricting its efforts to curb the deficit to relatively marginal influences. The deficit has not been allowed to hamstring the institution of economic policies which were in themselves desirable. The commitment to reduced unemployment and to faster rates of economic growth was made in 1961, and economic policies were bent toward achieving a satisfactory state of affairs domestically. As the economy began to achieve more closely its economic potential, the increased domestic activity engendered increased imports. In

141

turn, the increase in imports required the invention and institution of even more defensive measures designed to protect the dollar.

The so-called dollar shortage was the result of a tremendous disruption in the economic framework underlying the world's international trade and capital markets. As this shortage worked itself out with the help of enlightened policies, it was only natural that the pendulum should swing past its equilibrium point and over to a position of dollar deficit in which the United States needs to seek credit from the very nations that had been in deficit. In an inherently stable economic world, the swings will slowly decrease until the deficits and surpluses of the dollar will comprise only minor oscillations around an equilibrium of approximate balance.[1] The dollar deficit is likely to prove to be a phenomenon of shorter duration than the dollar shortage (except that the period of shortage was reduced by means of capital controls and a whole host of postwar controls which are currently neither available nor acceptable). But the dollar deficit has lasted too long. The reason for these long periods of disequilibrium is the negation of the corrective forces of the marketplace by national governments devoted primarily to the achievement of domestic economic goals. These domestic commitments have excluded the use of flexible rates of exchange as a clearing device in foreign exchange markets, of frequent small depreciations or appreciations of currencies in order to substitute for the absence of flexible rates, and of the use of interest rate policy as a means of achieving an inflow of capital or reducing an outflow. Income and employment adjustments are ruled out by postwar standards of governmental economic responsibilities. Long periods of adjustment have been unavoidable after a disturbance of the magnitude of the Second World War. The rigidities of the system suggest that a recurrence of a period of strain for nondollar nations may soon be the feature of the world economy as the pendulum overswings its mark again.

Hopefully any further swings in the balance of payments will not necessitate significant social costs of adjustment. There are three distinct reasons for optimism: (1) The nations which will be in deficit when the United States reverts to a surplus will have a store of liquid reserves which they have accumulated during the dollar deficit. If these reserves are used, the adjustment can be made gradually and

[1] This estimate was made prior to the payments strains imposed by the increased effort in S.E. Asia.

with minimal social costs. (2) The developed nations of the world are aware of the need for an increased supply of international liquidity to be available to nations whose international accounts are in deficit. (3) The experience gained in the last twenty years has enabled economists, central bankers and politicians to gain a familiarity with the workings of the world of international trade and finance after a long period when international trade was minimal because of a world conflict, a world depression and a slow recovery from the two catastrophes. This experience has . . . produced a greater awareness of the interdependency of nations for economic health.

Vital to diminishing the next swing of the pendulum is the need for the United States and other developed nations quickly to recognize, and if possible, to foresee, the end of the period of dollar deficit. Once the change has been recognized, the governments must institute measures to assist the system to right itself, or, at least, to avoid aggravating the imbalance by too slow a reaction to the new circumstances. In international finance the readjustment to a new situation will be more quickly made, and less painfully achieved, if both deficit and surplus nations react to the imbalance. Unfortunately there is a mistaken aura of virtue in being a surplus nation. This virtue together with the inconvenience and possible real costs (in terms of domestic goals) of helping to restore an international equilibrium, and the lack of any urgent pressure to take constructive steps, usually means that the burden of adjustment to the imbalance is necessarily made by the deficit nation. Such a unilateral policy almost inevitably entails greater social costs than would a policy of joint action.

There is a further danger. Since World War II, the nations of the world have been attempting, with some degree of success, to reduce the restrictions on international trade which existed in the immediate postwar years. The most well-known avenue is the series of negotiations held under the General Agreement on Tariffs and Trade. Progress on this front has, to some extent, been negated by impediments to trade and investment invoked by the United States in defense of the dollar. It is quite possible that some of these barriers may be more difficult to eliminate than they were to impose. If these defenses are not dismantled when a surplus is achieved, then nations which have seen their own surpluses turn into deficits will, in turn, seek to erect their own impediments. Thus, the world will have instigated a set of barriers to trade which largely offset each other, as a result of a complete cycle of payments imbalances. Optimal policy therefore requires that the United States, when she achieves a surplus, must quickly dismantle her restrictions. Some measures have only temporary political authority and these may be expected not to be renewed. However, these are mostly restraints on capital account. The elimination of other measures, especially those which affect current account transactions (e.g., government purchases of goods and services) will encounter strong resistance.

It is both theoretically correct and practically desirable that the definition of elimination of the deficit necessarily involves the removal of the temporary restrictions. The first step toward eliminating the deficit will occur when the United States achieves a balance on international account within the existing framework of restrictions. (If the fluctuations in economic activity are out-of-phase, it will not be necessary for a booming United States to achieve a strict balance since some allowance can be made for the reduction in imports attributable to the recession in Western Europe. However, it is likely that native caution will require that a strict balance be achieved for a respectable period of time—say, an average balance on the official settlements concept over a four-quarter period.) Once this first-stage balance has been attained, however, it must not be viewed or proclaimed as a true balance. A true balance will have been attained only when the temporary restrictions and the deficit have been simultaneously eliminated.

The definition of balance as existing when restrictions to American imports have been reduced to the level prevailing in, say 1958, will help guard against two undesirable possibilities: (1) The failure of the United States to assist the newly deficit nations in the adjustment process; and (2) an increase in the overall level of restrictions on international trade and investment.

International trade is undertaken to promote the welfare of the people of the world. This benefit can be eroded by the unnecessary social costs incurred if nations fail to help each other in the adjustment process which is necessary after structural change takes place. Because of its huge wealth and stock of liquid reserves the United States was able to survive a prolonged dollar deficit without resort to drastic measures and the consequent infliction of drastic social costs. It is equally important that these social costs be kept at a minimum when the deficit has been removed since the social costs are nearly always borne by the weak: the marginal worker and the poor country.

SUGGESTIONS FOR READING

There are at least four volumes which devote themselves almost exclusively to consideration of the causes and cures of the dollar deficit. Excerpts from these volumes have been included in this volume or are mentioned below, but all four can be recommended to the serious student in their entirety: Walter S. Salant and Associates, *The United States Balance of Payments in 1968* (Washington, D.C., 1963); *Factors Affecting the United States Balance of Payments*, Joint Economic Committee compilation of studies: 87th Congress, 2nd Session (December 14, 1962); *The Dollar in Crisis*, ed. Seymour E. Harris (New York, 1962); and the Symposium in Honor of Seymour E. Harris: "The United States Balance of Payments and the World Payments Mechanism," *The Review of Economics and Statistics*, XLVI (May 1964).

On the measurement of the balance of payments see: *The Balance of Payments Statistics of the United States, A Review and Appraisal*, Report of the Review Committee for Balance of Payments Statistics to the Bureau of the Budget (Washington, D.C., 1965), in particular Chapter IX, which is concerned with the actual definition of the deficit; Harry G. Johnson, "The International Competitive Position of the United States and the Balance of Payments for 1968," *The Review of Economics and Statistics*, XLVI (February 1964); and Peter B. Kenen, "Measuring the United States Balance of Payments," *The Review of Economics and Statistics*, XLVI (May 1964).

The causes of the deficit are treated in John E. Floyd, "The Overvaluation of the Dollar," *American Economic Review*, LV (March 1965); Lawrence B. Krause, "Import Discipline: The Case of the United States Steel Industry," *The Journal of Industrial Economics*, XI (November 1962); Irving B. Kravis, "The U.S. Trade Position and the Common Market," in *Factors Affecting the United States Balance of Payments*; Charles S. Murphy, "United States Agricultural Exports and the European Common Market" in *Outlook for United States Balance of Payments*, Hearings before the Subcommittee on International Exchange and Payments of the Joint Economic Committee, December 1962 (U.S. Government Printing Office). Reprinted in *The Common Market: Progress and Controversy*, ed. Lawrence B. Krause (Englewood Cliffs, N. J., 1964); and Walter S. Salant, "Recent Developments in Factors Affecting the United States Basic Balance of Payments," *Weltwirtschaftliches Archiv* (Heft 2, 1964).

For the debate over alternative cures of the deficit see: Richard E. Caves, "Flexible Exchange Rates," *The American Economic Review*, LIII (May 1963); Harry G. Johnson, "Equilibrium Under Fixed Exchange Rates," *The American Economic Review*, LIII (May 1963); Peter B. Kenen, *Giant Among Nations* (New York, 1963); Alexander Lamfalussy, "The Thirty-five Dollar Question," *Lloyds Bank Review* (October 1963); Fritz Machlup, "Plans for Reform of the International Monetary System," Special Papers in International Economics, No. 3 (Princeton, 1964); Warren Smith, "Are There Enough Policy Tools?," *The American Economic Review*, LV (May 1965); and Paul Wonnacott, "A Suggestion for the Revaluation of Gold," *The Journal of Finance*, XVIII (March 1963).